The Disruptive Volunteer Manager

A step-by-step guide to reshaping non-profit culture, redefining volunteers as volunteer investors, redefining volunteer managers as leaders of volunteers, reframing priorities for maximum impact, reframing volunteer retention as sustainability and re-imagining the future.

Meridian Swift

Dedication: To all those who work alongside volunteers and who give of their time and talents to make our communities better.

Meridian Swift
Copyright   2019:   ISBN 9781976069314

Table of Contents

Foreword. 5

The Pre-Step: Rethinking Ourselves 7

Step 1: Reframing Volunteer Management 13

Step 2: Redefining the Volunteer Role 29

Step 3: Redefining the Volunteer Manager Role. 57

Step 4: Reframing Priorities and Vision. 87

Step 5: Reframing Retention 123

Step 6: Re-imagining the Future 163

Foreword

I've loved everything about managing volunteers. I've loved watching volunteers' faces when they realize how much their care meant to someone who was hurting. I've loved seeing people helped by the gentle touch of a volunteer who was present and in the moment. I've loved seeing volunteers find something wonderfully new and profound about themselves. I've even loved the challenges because working with volunteers weaves this rich tapestry of life events.

But, after spending years working with volunteers and creating volunteer engagement programs, it occurred to me while the world around was changing, managing volunteers remained stuck in an outdated paradigm. It didn't match the incredible work my volunteers were doing.

If we wish to engage modern volunteers and celebrate all they bring, then we need to readjust our methods to best meet the needs of a changing volunteer landscape. We need to move volunteer organizations into a new normal, one that places volunteerism front and center.

While researching and working with organizations, clients, volunteers and volunteer managers, it became clear to me: There is a gap in the volunteerism world. The gap lies between the hands-on engagement of volunteers and the control of volunteerism's direction.

Who better knows the needs of volunteers? Who better knows the capabilities of volunteers? Who better knows the roles volunteers want and can excel at, beyond the wildest expectations of any organization? Who better knows how to keep volunteers coming back?

That's right. The Volunteer Manager. It is the volunteer manager who invests time in the volunteer, seeks to learn why a volunteer stays and who spends evenings on the phone with a volunteer who just lost a loved one.

If there is one thing I hope you take away from this book, it is the sense that by becoming proactive and taking control of your volunteer program, you will elevate your volunteers and your standing within your organization.

There's no law requiring volunteer managers to feel as though we are hamsters on a wheel forever running. Becoming a leader of volunteers means investing in yourself, your abilities and your vision. It means influencing your organization to embrace volunteerism in the ways you demonstrate are most beneficial to accomplishing mission goals. My hope is these six steps resonate with you and you feel as though you can implement some or all in a way that works for your program. I hope that you will realize your potential and recognize your critical role in furthering volunteerism.

Success is often equated with the loudest voices getting what they want. But do demanding voices enact a change with roots? Our goal as leaders of volunteers is to enact sustainable volunteerism, so it better serves our clients, our volunteers and our organizations. It is the unwavering, professional volunteer manager voice that will reframe volunteer management by redefining volunteers, reshaping non-profit culture and re-imagining the future. By first changing ourselves and our approach, we will usher in system-wide changes.

I am writing this book for you, whether you're a new volunteer manager, or have been in this field for years. Our profession is essential to a caring, involved society. We can and must take control of our programs, one step at a time so we can move them into the modern world where they will flourish. We must increase our influence to strengthen volunteerism and to change the world for the better. Together, we can do this.

-Meridian

The Pre-Step: Rethinking Ourselves

Charles called the number listed on the volunteer wanted ad. The coordinator who answered the phone was warm and friendly. She invited him to come to the next open house for volunteers.

That Friday afternoon, Charles arrived, eager to get started for a cause he believed in. He sat near the back of the room and looked around at the diverse group of people finding their seats. The coordinator stepped to the front and thanked everyone for coming. She gave a short history of her organization, then explained the program along with the training required while she wrote the available jobs on the whiteboard. She paused for questions.

"I'm interested in the data specialist position," a woman in the front row said. "Can I show up when I have some extra time?"

"Well, not for this job." The coordinator pointed at the schedule. "We need someone to come in on a regular basis."

"I have a son who is in a soccer league," a man in back raised his hand. "Do you have something his group can do?"

"Um, maybe. It depends upon what we might put together. You can see me later and we can talk."

The young woman in front of Charles spoke up. "I have experience in advertising. Is there something I can do to help the marketing department?"

"Well," the coordinator replied, "I can check with that department later. Right now they have no jobs listed. Do you think you could volunteer in our office until something comes up?"

Charles tentatively raised his hand. "I have an idea for a campaign that might bring in extra donations. I've worked this program before at my company and it was pretty successful. I thought it would be nice to share it with you."

The volunteer coordinator smiled wistfully. "We can certainly discuss your idea at some point. Right now though, we have to get back to the roles we need." The coordinator paused for a moment and looked at the hopeful faces. Their enthusiasm and potential shimmered in front of her, a ghost of what could be. She sighed. "Now, who can come in on Thursday afternoons?"

Every day, people are searching for ways to be of service. They help a neighbor in need. They donate money to a cause they believe will change the world for the better. They read articles on becoming kinder versions of themselves. They contact organizations and offer to volunteer their time and talents.

Are we serving their needs? Are we providing the best volunteer experience for our volunteers or can we do better? Are we losing the opportunity to engage good people because we are stuck in an outmoded volunteer management system?

Are we robbing people of the incredible benefits volunteering offers them because we view ourselves as simply coordinators, bound to fill tasks when we know how much more our volunteers are capable of?

Walk down the sidewalk of almost any major city in the world. What do you see on the bustling streets and in the gleaming buildings? You see signs of progress everywhere. Progress is the constant change moving us forward as we adapt to shifting landscapes.

As you walk down the sidewalk, you won't see a wagon wheel repair shop in modern cities because progress has rendered those shops obsolete. The wagon wheel repair owners who, over time watched the rise of the automobile, either learned how to fix tires or they went out of business.

Is volunteer management stuck in the wagon wheel repair shop era? Are we watching progress pass us by while we struggle to keep an antiquated system afloat?

What do we need to do to bring volunteerism and leading volunteers into modern times?

In this book, we will examine how traditional thinking about volunteers and volunteer management is as outmoded as wagon wheel repair shops. We will lay out a proactive plan to initiate change, by instituting a step-by-step process to redefine and reframe volunteer management. Each step builds on the one before it.

These changes cannot be accomplished in a day or a week, but are designed for the long haul. If we wish to disrupt the entrenched norm, then we must prepare to build a new normal, one positive step at a time.

Each step organically leads to the next one and adds to the one before it. Disrupting the status quo is always a challenge when you are the one who sees the need for change.

Have you heard these complaints: "I can never get a volunteer when I need one," or "you say we have 50 volunteers, how is it possible that none of them is available tomorrow night?" If senior management see problems as shortcomings on the volunteer manager's part, instead of as symptoms of a failed system, change is much harder to implement. Are we stuck?

We first must ask, how does non-profit organizational culture view the contributions of volunteers and volunteer management? Do staff cheerfully say, "we couldn't do this without our volunteers," or "our volunteers are the extra layer of caring?" We must look past the phrases that have become standard fare and examine the culture. Are volunteers fully integrated into organizations?

Fully integrated means viewing volunteers as partners with staff. It means courting volunteers for their skills, recognizing them for their contributions and including them in mission planning. It means non-profit staff feel the benefits of engaging volunteers. It means volunteer achievements are front and center on organizational press releases, marketing material and websites. It means volunteer department budgets are on a par with other departments. It means investing in the education and management training for the volunteer manager is considered an investment in organizational success.

It means volunteer managers are part of senior management. It means volunteer managers are always part of the planning process and any new project involving volunteers is subject to volunteer manager input.

If we wish to see volunteerism take its rightful place in the non-profit world, we must reframe organizational culture. Convincing non-profit hearts and minds that the volunteer management system is outdated will not be easy. We have to approach it one beneficial step at a time.

Let's be honest. Staff may view volunteer involvement as a nuisance, or a job threat or something they have no time for. I remember a staff member saying to me, after I shared an intimate moment between a client and a volunteer, "yeah, your volunteers get all the meaty stuff. You don't think I'd like to get the chance to connect with clients? I'm stuck doing my job."

How does staff view volunteers? Staff may be uncomfortable and think volunteers are looking over their shoulders. They may feel threatened by a skilled volunteer and think the volunteer wants to take their job. They may be a bit jealous and look at volunteers as getting all the prime assignments while they have to do the boring stuff, like filling out paperwork or going to endless meetings.

The deep, systemic changes must speak to the benefit for all. Embracing the reframing of volunteer management must be perceived as a win-win for our organizations or else they will view us as nothing more than shrill complainers, negative thinkers, or disgruntled staff members unable to do the job.

But if we can show how rethinking volunteers, volunteer management and volunteer managers is a leap forward and a benefit to not only organizational missions but also to staff, then we can succeed. We have a tremendous opportunity in front of us.

Each step is designed to disrupt the ingrained norm with a focus on a professional remaking of ourselves and our programs. Why remake ourselves?

When I left my job to focus on writing and helping other volunteer managers, I was somewhat burned out. I'd instituted programs, some that won awards, on-boarded thousands of capable volunteers, ethically mediated challenges and put organizational needs ahead of my own. But I felt that so much of my job was misunderstood.

One day, I was talking to a wise friend about volunteer management. I told her volunteer managers are some of the most misunderstood and under-appreciated people in the non-profit world.

"Uh huh." She said. "Is this really about all the other volunteer managers out there?"

"Well, yes. I've heard it from so many that I've worked with since I left my job. It's a common theme. No one understands us."

She raised an eyebrow. "And what did you do to make them understand?"

"Everything. I told them about the things volunteers want and need, about the important work volunteers are doing. They just didn't get it."

"What did you want them to do, these people that didn't understand? Fundamentally, I mean."

"I wanted them to change."

"Oh," she said. "Then maybe you needed to change first."

That hit me hard. Me change? Why? I thought I did everything right in my job, yet I felt misunderstood. What more could I have done? But yet, something about what she said tugged at me. Was she right? Did I internalize everything?

I began to look at volunteer management differently. Were my expectations of staff too one-sided? Did I think the things obvious to me were obvious to everyone else? What could I have done differently to explain volunteer management?

It was one of those light-bulb moments. I realized that frustrations kept me from seeing a clear picture. In the non-profit world, everyone's job is stressful.

We all feel the acute pressure of helping others. Sure, we experience helper's high, but we also experience the pressure of meeting deadlines, properly documenting work, staying within budget guidelines, mitigating risk and battling for limited resources. It's no wonder one staff member has no time nor emotional energy to understand the challenges facing another staff member, much less the nuances of managing volunteers.

If we wish to disrupt the system, the first thing we must do is disrupt ourselves. We must adjust our approach from within and change the way we operate. We must make it our priority to form a new normal in how organizations view our volunteers and how we, volunteer managers are perceived.

All those hours we spend learning about volunteers, understanding their motivations and encouraging their capabilities is a bubble of possibilities waiting to burst open. Our input in shaping volunteerism will unleash the potential to help the non-profit world accomplish even greater objectives.

We can control the outcome if we are proactive. You see, control always exists. If we don't take control of volunteering's direction, its control will reside with others. The onus is on us to take control, professionalize our approach and then show others the worth of our professional programs.

Taking control also means taking control of our view. In place of viewing challenges, let's view opportunities. We have the opportunity to remake perceptions of volunteering which as a result, will advance and increase it. Let's start with reframing non-profit culture.

Step 1: Reframing Volunteer Management and Reshaping Non-Profit Culture

A long time ago, I went to my first conference featuring a volunteer track. I took my seat amongst my peers, eager to learn more about this exciting field. Sitting next to me was a woman dressed in a business suit, busily writing in her notebook. Oh, I thought, she must be an executive. How wonderful it was that she wanted to learn more about volunteering and its benefits. After a few moments, she looked up and around at the people filtering in. She peered at all the casual outfits and turned to me.

"Is this meeting room A7?"

"No," I said, this is A5, the volunteer presentation."

"I see," she closed her notebook and got up. "I'm in the wrong place. I need to be in the professional development presentation."

If we want the non-profit world to take us seriously and acknowledge our volunteers' contributions, then we must stop looking at what we do as a job. Instead, we must view ourselves as professionals. We must take our rightful place among clinical staff, marketers and administration.

But how? Where do we turn? There is no playbook, no definitive guide on how to become a volunteer management professional so where should we look for advice on reframing volunteer management and reshaping non-profit culture? Is there a magical formula we need to follow?

Strategizing a professional approach does not mean that we must forgo the touchy-feely parts of volunteer management. Think about the teaching profession. Teachers are widely viewed as caring people who prepare young minds for the future.

Just because we strive for respect and understanding doesn't mean we must become cold and unapproachable. It doesn't mean we have to reduce our volunteers down to numbers and ignore the intangible goodness we witness daily.

It means we have to remake ourselves into leaders of a movement. It means we have to redefine our volunteers and rework our methods of showing value and impact.

Let's learn from successful professions outside our non-profit world by turning to business, marketing and even science for tools to help us. We need not invent anything. But what we need to do is to adopt and adapt successful components from the private sector and retool them in ways that work for us.

Step 1 is acknowledging the urgent need to reframe volunteerism and volunteer management and reshape non-profit culture. The world is in fluid movement. People are changing, society is evolving, and the importance of technology in our lives is growing. The question then becomes, what effect does each of these three changing landscapes have on volunteering and volunteer management?

People: Modern businesses realize an authoritarian management approach doesn't work anymore. Savvy business leaders understand their employees contribute skills and knowledge which increases productivity and leads to higher profits. Workers are **human capital,** a term describing the value each worker adds to a company. In place of characterizing employees as replaceable tools, human capital redefines employees as unique individuals that contribute.

By studying motivation and skills utilization, employee retention, cost of onboarding new employees versus keeping established ones, pay versus meaningful work and team building, companies are learning how to get the most from their people. We can borrow this term and call it **volunteer capital**.

Volunteers are changing because people are changing. In step 2, we will see how modern volunteers differ from volunteers of the past and we will redefine their role.

Society is evolving: Volunteering does not happen in a vacuum. It is part of the fabric of civilized society. We help one another. We feel empathy for our fellow man. Society is becoming more attuned to the plight of friends and neighbors.

On the surface, one might expect that because we are becoming more cognizant of societal problems, volunteering would naturally increase but that's not true. Volunteerism is ripe for expansion but it's not expanding at the rate it should be, at least not in traditionally measured ways. Why? Because the system in place frustrates volunteers, even though it served their counterparts in the past.

Technology is expanding: Only fifty years ago local newspapers, conversations over the back fence and the fifteen minute news broadcast on one of just a few television networks shaped our opinions. Today, instant news and opinions from social media inundate us with a 24-hour cycle.

A generation ago we waited to get home to make a phone call on our land line. We wrote letters to one another. We saved up communication until we could get in touch with someone. Today, communication is instantaneous.

Technology plays an enormous role in managing volunteers. Keeping up with advancing technology is necessary to recruiting, training and engaging today's volunteers. A few of the basic changes in the past years include:
- Search engines find volunteer opportunities.
- Paper volunteer job applications are online applications.
- Phone calls are texts or emails.
- Sign-up sheets are online.
- Volunteers share comments on social media.
- Websites answer frequently asked questions.
- Volunteers find testimonials on social media sites.
- Volunteers fill virtual tasks.

We have to move forward to keep up. Planting the seeds of change lays the foundation for the following steps. It means realizing the frustrations surrounding volunteer management are not because of any personal failure, but due to the stagnation in this field. The frustrations we, volunteer managers are feeling stem from working within a system not adequately updated to meet modern volunteer needs.

Step 1 is unleashing the will to disrupt the system.

We can start by examining why volunteer managers feel frustrated. What creates feelings of frustration? Staff not understanding the nuances of volunteer motivation? Tasks which demean a volunteer's abilities? Disregard for a volunteer's time? Last-minute requests? A never ending volunteer recruitment cycle? These frustrations are all examples of how the outdated volunteer management system impedes our ability to succeed.

I've met so many volunteer managers weary of trying to make antiquated processes work. I remember a conversation I had with a manager who told me, "I love what I do. I get excited when I send a volunteer to help a person because I know that in my own way, I've contributed to something meaningful. I just wish I could make others see what I do in the way I see it."

Can you imagine a world in which we, volunteer managers could have it all? In this world, we get to do all the meaningful parts of our jobs such as seeing volunteers flourish, creating roles for talented volunteers and enhancing a client's life, but as a bonus, we receive respect as professionals with sharply honed skills. In this world, we plan volunteer engagement. In this world we have leverage for budgeting and professional development.

This world can exist if we are hungry enough for it and have the will to change our approach. Once we have the will for reframing volunteer management, then we can bring our organizations onboard with new methods designed for results. Implementing change is hard work.

It takes conviction and a resolve stemming from knowing what you are doing is the right thing to do, not only for the volunteers, but for the organization and yourself.

And here's another reason for us to develop the will to disrupt: Each other. We owe every volunteer manager today and those who will come after us, our concerted effort to enact change. We owe one another the rising tide of professionalism that will lift all boats.

Where do you think a CEO gets general information on volunteer management? Mainly from other executives when they attend meetings or conferences or chat on the phone. They are asking one another and not volunteer engagement experts.

So, take a moment and think about what your CEO or Executive Director will say about you and your volunteer engagement program when conversing with another executive. He or she might say something like, "It's good, and we like our volunteers. Our coordinator does a good job; the volunteers seem happy."

Disrupting means hearing your Executive Director say, "our volunteer initiative is amazing. Our volunteers' impact is felt in every mission area and we are expanding their role." Disrupting means organizations are excited about their volunteer programs and seek volunteer manager input.

Step 1 is looking at the bigger picture. We must convey the importance of volunteer contributions so our organizations understand and by understanding, find value. We must be able to articulate and frame the nuanced work we do daily to engage volunteers. We must at all times convey a professional, goal and solution-oriented, mission centric attitude.

Step 1 is putting emotions aside. Once you commit to disrupt, it is imperative you remove any personal emotions from each step. Demanding change because you are feeling hurt, or ignored, or fed up does not lay a solid foundation. Personal feelings cloud judgment. Personal feelings color the way we view results. Personal feelings blind us to the bigger picture.

Elevating volunteer management and updating the system takes discipline and an unbiased eye. It takes the will to step away emotionally and examine things from a logical perspective. It means learning to always act professionally and to become results-oriented. It takes a proactive approach.

How we broach change is key. For every argument we offer championing change, there will be an opposing view. Simply announcing the way the non-profit world views volunteers and volunteer programs is outdated will fail miserably.

An opposing view will counter with, "why change, things are fine," or "nothing's perfect, and besides, we're too busy to change," or "you're unhappy. Please, just do your job or go somewhere else."

Step 1 means collaborating, not opposing. If we appear to have a chip on our shoulders, we will fail. An emotionally charged atmosphere in which staff and senior management push back against changes will generate an impossible uphill battle. It is imperative staff and senior management feel they are a contributing partner with you when starting any changes.

Rely on all those highly sharpened people skills when approaching the steps to reframing and redefining. Use the same persuasive techniques you use with volunteers. Think of the last time you had to introduce change to your volunteers. What did you tell them? I'll bet you didn't say, "Hey, the old way stinks, so we will do it this way now."

Take into consideration the emotions staff and senior management will feel when suggesting the old way of managing volunteers is no longer working. They may feel you are pointing a finger at them and the way they view volunteering. Their perception that you are equating change with a shortcoming on their part can impede your message.

Think about it this way. We own our work. We own the way we do things and anyone who challenges the way we do things is subtly challenging us and our judgment.

We have to contend with and overcome the ownership of the old norm in the way things are run. Any suggestion implying the norm is not working is a subtle criticism of everyone operating under that norm. And this tiny nuance is the area in which your message can fall flat. It's the **no-change zone**.

Go back to how you introduce change to your volunteers and borrow those well thought out methods and apply them in this scenario. Be ready to field extensive feedback from staff and be prepared to accept suggestions and criticisms with the same gracious attitude you exhibit towards your volunteers. Be ready to adjust your expectations and tweak outcomes to court buy-in from staff.

Messages aimed at staff must speak to their needs. Saying, "I've got this volunteer here to help you," doesn't address staff objections, whether spoken or unspoken. As we prepare to disrupt and reframe, we must understand the need to have staff onboard. We must get inside their heads and feel their feelings so we can work with them and not against them.

Our organizational cultures are at play. Organizations write mission statements to define their reason to exist. We share the reality of the work.

But internal cultures develop over time that stray far from the mission. Organizations are comprised of people who may backstab, point fingers, lash out when stressed, play favorites and demean others. When we, volunteer managers step outside inner workings and present a return to a shared reality, one that harkens back to the "why," we will be heard.

Organizations can devolve into processes and easily lose the "why we do what we do." Our opportunity lies in returning to the why, in getting excited about the reasons our organizations were formed in the first place. Volunteers embody the spirit of the why. They come, not looking to be mired in the minutia, but eager to contribute to our missions. This is where the organizational heart beats and by elevating volunteerism, we will lift everyone.

Let's be realistic. Influencing opinions is much easier if opinions are not yet formed. Think of a time you pitched a new volunteer initiative to senior management. Their minds were at least open to hearing new ideas whether or not they accepted your proposal.

Disrupting the old order is much harder. Opinions have already been formed and changing made up minds will take tact, consistency and calm patience. You must deeply believe in the worth of the direction you are taking your organization because it won't happen overnight.

Remind staff that volunteers do not want to take jobs from them nor come to find fault. Reassure staff that volunteers think non-profit staff members are unsung heroes who work tirelessly to make this world a better place.

Step 1 is laying a foundation for creating a new normal, a normal that breaks the barriers keeping us stuck. The embedded, though outdated volunteer management system has produced a weird, dysfunctional balance within the non-profit sector. Picture a teeter totter or seesaw in your mind with the volunteer manager on one end, senior management and key staff on the other. Now picture volunteer engagement in the middle.

In the past, the more we, volunteer managers scrambled to fill tasks designed by senior management and key staff, the lower we sunk on the seesaw while senior management and key staff rose.

The more we shied away from taking control of our programs, the more control went to others while volunteer engagement's direction was removed from us.

And because we felt let down by this out of whack balancing act, we became frustrated to the point where some volunteer managers wanted to jump off the seesaw and watch senior management crash. It's time to remove looking at administration and key staff as opposition and instead, balance our seesaw as equal partners in volunteer engagement.

We want our organizations to embrace volunteers so it is up to us to put aside our emotions and put our passions into building bridges. It is up to us to be the bigger person and put furthering volunteerism ahead of any perceived personal slights or misunderstandings.

Step 1 is enlisting allies who have buy-in. Applaud staff and share the positive things volunteers say about them. Reiterate that volunteers want to support their hard-work and often place staff on a pedestal.

Interview staff and ask them what type of volunteer help they would welcome and what qualities they would like to see in their volunteers. By asking them to make a "**wish list**" for volunteer skills and temperament, you will establish their future participation.

Take the information and apply it when placing volunteers by using a **trio of reinforcements**. The first reinforcement emphasizes the wish list items you've gotten from the staff member.

The second is to add in a compliment and the third is the implied expectation that the staff member will mentor the volunteer. Let's look at how the trio is applied.

Staff member Juan asks for a volunteer to help him make follow-up phone calls. In Juan's **wish list interview**, he said he would prefer a volunteer who doesn't need a lot of extensive handholding.

You assign a volunteer to him and say, "Juan, you asked for a volunteer to help you make phone calls. I have a new volunteer Sal, who has corporate experience, and he doesn't need a great deal of instruction, something you mentioned would be a helpful quality. With your extensive knowledge (compliment) and expert guidance (expectation), Sal can free up the time you need to spend doing the tasks you must get done."

Always assure staff they have options. Let them know everything volunteer related is subject to their satisfaction and you are there to support them. Sometimes staff can feel as though volunteers are forced upon them and then they will subconsciously reject the volunteer before she even starts. Acknowledging staff's right to be dissatisfied gives them the control they need.

Tell them, "I will periodically check in on volunteer Betty. If, for any reason, there is a problem or an issue, please let me know. Betty is here to help you and she is eager to take a portion of your workload off of you. She does not want to add to your responsibilities, but wishes to help you be more productive."

Ask staff to help you craft your volunteer policies and procedures and encourage them to give their input on volunteer behavior "no-nos." Thank staff for their valuable input and use the feedback when onboarding volunteers.

Step 1 is using marketing. We can borrow marketing strategies to "sell" our volunteer engagement initiative.

Companies spend a great deal of time and effort trying to understand the consumer so they can successfully market their products. There's no reason we can't view our organizations as our customers as we market the value of our volunteers. What does our customer want?

What do they need and what is valuable to them? Is it time? We can use that to our advantage and say, "our volunteers will free up your time." Is it less work? We can market to that need by saying, "our volunteers will take some of the workload off of you."

Companies have this marketing trick. When selling products or subscription services, they routinely offer three product options. Watch the next advertisement for a subscription service. It will invariably contain three options. One of those options serves to steer consumers to the option the company wants you to purchase. It works because the option they want you to buy looks like a bargain compared to the one known as the "decoy option," which is constructed to be less valuable.

How can this concept work for volunteer management? It works because you can offer staff and senior management options, which is a simple premise that allows staff and upper management to exercise control over a choice which makes them more likely to participate.

Instead of saying, "I want to make these changes," you offer options for change. You say, "I have three options and I want you, staff or senior management team, to tell me which one you're comfortable with."

Give three workable options so the one they choose is one you can live with. If you really want to drive their choice to one particular option, then add consequences to each one. Consequences will help determine which option is the most desirable.

For example, let's say your volunteers have been telling you they wish staff would get more involved with appreciation events. So, you approach senior management. Instead of saying, "Look, the volunteers are unhappy because they feel as though staff is ignoring them and not taking part in appreciation events," you approach with a positive message and offer three options.

You say, "I'd like to revamp our volunteer appreciation event. Our volunteers have voiced they would love to mingle with staff because volunteers have told me how much it means to them when staff acknowledges them. Here are three ideas I have for revamping the volunteer luncheon."

- We keep the volunteer luncheon, but we have to spend more money so all staff can come. It will mean virtually closing down for an afternoon.

- We do away with the volunteer luncheon and instead ask staff to do a cookout for the volunteers on a Saturday. It will mean paying staff to come in on Saturday and asking them to bring a dish. It might disrupt their weekend plans, however.

- We host a breakfast at our monthly staff meeting and invite the volunteers to attend. They will feel that staff is acknowledging them as members of the team because staff has invited them.

During the meeting we can say thank you to the volunteers and I can get a caterer to supply the food. It would cost less than the luncheon, but it would mean forgoing the meeting agenda just this one time so we could focus on the volunteers.

There's nothing wrong with offering options when asking for changes. Offering options costing more money or disrupting workflow highlights your third option which shows a willingness to enact a change embracing fiscal responsibility and consideration for staff. After all, you could actually ask for outrageous changes, but you're not. And you're giving control of the final decision to senior management as an incentive.

Step 1 is creating an atmosphere ripe for change. When introducing a new normal, repeat key messages with confidence and frame the change message into how much the staff and organization will benefit. Be prepared for give and take. Allow for opposing ideas to challenge your claims. Be willing to compromise and seek the greater good over getting your way.

Give staff credit. Highlight staff contributions. Mention them by name when speaking of successes. Offer awards for staff instrumental in implementing your steps. The more we treat them as partners in modern volunteer engagement, the more staff will want to partner with us.

So, what do we call this first stage? Partnering in Change? A Change Collaborative? Even the word change can have a negative connotation. Change implies something is broken, or something is wrong.

Think of the subtle marketing strategies companies use to imply a positive change without using the word: Build, Grow, Succeed, or Plant. These words convey a sense of working towards a desirable outcome, of building upon something, or moving forward without implicitly criticizing the status quo.

Step 1 is choosing words carefully for maximum impact. Forget "we must change," and incorporate "**we are building an exceptional volunteer engagement program (or initiative).**" Use phrases implying expectations to come, such as "**positioning for the future,**" or "**cultivating quality,**" or "**planting the seeds of excellence.**"

Start a buzz. Drop teasers suggesting you are studying volunteerism trends and practices. Broadcast your plan to make your volunteer engagement initiative a cutting edge model that will be the envy of other organizations.

Refer to the expanding world of knowledge and your desire to position your organization as a trendsetter. Use phrases underlining the benefits of forward thinking. Make it clear you desire to improve your volunteer program to help the organizational mission succeed and help support the staff in accomplishing their goals.

Be the positive person in the room. Staff will listen to you talk about a change emphasizing a desire to move forward, to improve, and to add value over messaging sounding negative or complaint oriented. Avoid giving the impression change is necessary because nothing is working, or no one understands. We must lay a positive, forward moving foundation to disrupt the old and create a new normal.

Step 1 is cultivating the expectation of great things to come. Not only will the repeated expression promising great things plant the seeds of change in the minds of staff and senior management, but it will serve as a motivating impetus for you to follow through.

Make change about your initiative. Explain that you are not asking staff to change, but that your program is changing to better meet organizational needs. Get excited.

People are not so keen to hear they need to change, but are very open to hearing about someone else making positive changes. As they embrace your positive changes, they will then change as a result. They will level out the seesaw.

I remember being frustrated with one staff member who never seemed to give clear directions to volunteers. I would politely ask her to be more specific when instructing volunteers but she would shrug and say, "It's really self-explanatory. I think they should be able to do simple data entry."

Volunteers continued to bemoan her lack of instruction. So one day, I said to her, "I heard what you said and from now on, I will send you only the volunteers who have had extensive experience in data entry."

She was taken aback, but pleased. And she changed. She spent more time with each volunteer, making sure they knew exactly how she wanted the job done. It worked because I changed my approach.

Disrupting the system is not a quick fix, but a steady and continual march to an end result. Enlist your volunteers in helping motivate you. Include them in this first stage by sharing your plans with them.

Again, verbiage is key. If you tell volunteers they will finally get their due, you will construct a counterproductive barrier between the volunteers and the organization. Avoid the "us versus them" trap.

Instead, tell volunteers you are on a **mission of value,** and with their help, you will establish a volunteer program they will be even more proud to serve. Compliment them and invite them to the future of volunteer engagement and ask them to partner with you in cultivating this future.

Use your **mission of value** as a recruitment tool. Enlist the volunteers in spreading the word your organization is positioning itself as a leader in volunteer engagement.

Step 1 is positioning yourself as the guide for the new normal. Volunteer managers are busy and strapped for time. Between recruiting, onboarding, assigning, mentoring and engaging volunteers, there is precious little time left for other tasks.

However, in order to reframe volunteer management and redefine volunteers and volunteer managers, carve out ample time to keep staff and senior management informed of your progress. Keep feeding enthusiasm and position yourself as the change leader.

At this point, you understandably are asking, "What will change? I already work well with my volunteers." Your work with volunteers which includes mentoring, coaching and matching will not change because it need not change. What does need to change is our place in the nonprofit world and how we show volunteer contributions. The 6 steps are designed to elevate volunteer management.

Implementing change is an investment in the long haul. Keep staff and management abreast of your successes so they can see your program's benefits. Repetition is critical. Repeating key phrases chips away at their formed perceptions and replaces them with your fresh ideas. It sets the new normal.

Keep staff interested by regularly communicating updates. Give your project a title. Naming an initiative something memorable like **"building the future of volunteer engagement project**," gives it an identity and a validity.

Always use the project name when referring to any updates and successes because repetition is key to absorbing new information and replacing old ideas with new ones. Schedule regular updates to keep the momentum going.

One convenient way to assure you have an audience is to ask if you can have a segment at staff meetings or at any mandatory events. Call it the "**building the future of volunteer engagement update**."

Piggy back five minutes of updates each time your organization conducts regularly scheduled meetings. Introduce new concepts or terminology, restate previous concepts, review new words and show successes in the form of statistics, volunteer stories, or testimonials from clients, volunteers or staff.

Repetition is key in creating the new normal. We retain information through repetition. It becomes ingrained. Our brains are computers, and repeating strengthens our long-term memory. While it may feel weird to say, "As I've shown before," or "as I said last time," it is a vital step to implanting a new direction, so repeat yourself often.

If you cannot do updates in person, then video is an option. Ask a volunteer to film you providing updates on your steps to reframing volunteer management. Staff will look forward to your videos if you inject humor and upbeat reporting. Try to make the updates fun because fun captures attention. Post them on your organization's internal shared drive.

If you have no access to video, or audio, then a quick newsletter will work nicely. Write a quick digital newsletter/news brief to distribute to staff and senior management highlighting the steps moving your volunteer initiative forward.

Highlighting success stories is incredibly motivating not only for the staff who read it, but for yourself as you chronicle the successful implementation of forward moving steps.

Step 1 means understanding the need for change, unleashing the will to change and positioning yourself as the change guide. Once you feel the surrounding atmosphere is alive with a positive charge and your organization is ready for you to lead the way to a new normal, then it is the right time to start implementing step 2.

Step 1 Checklist:
✓ Acknowledge the urgent need to reframe and reshape
✓ Unleash the will to disrupt the system
✓ Remember the bigger picture
✓ Put emotions aside
✓ Employ a collaborative effort
✓ Lay the foundation for a new normal
✓ Enlist allies who have buy-in
✓ Use marketing
✓ Create an atmosphere for change
✓ Choose words for maximum impact
✓ Cultivate an expectation of things to come
✓ Be the guide to a new normal
✓ Understand, unleash and position

Step 2: Redefining the Volunteer Role

Leta wasn't sure what to expect. Her 'Human Behavior in Society' class required five hours of community service and she had signed up to help run the kiddie dash at a local charity walk/run. It was her first volunteer event. When she arrived that morning, she approached the sign-in tent and found a woman wearing the event t-shirt barking orders at two other people. After the two hurried off, Leta cautiously approached.

"Hi, I'm Leta, I'm supposed to help with the kiddie dash."

"Oh," the women said, checking her clipboard. "Yes, I have you here." She peered over her glasses at Leta. "You know what? I had two friends sign up to help last minute, and I sent them over to do the kiddie dash. So, for you," the woman tapped her pencil on the clipboard, "you're young. I think I'll send you inside to fetch bottled water. Just go into the kitchen and someone in there will show you where it is. We need to keep the water supply filled." The women turned away.

"But," Leta said to the woman's back. "Sorry, but I signed up to work with the kids. It's a requirement for my college class. My professor specifically told us to volunteer with people. I have to do a report on it."

The woman turned back. "Look, maybe later you can pass the candy jar around to the kids. Right now I need you to bring the bottled water out here to this tent."

Why does the prevailing wisdom at most organizations assume volunteers have not changed in the past years, yet society and clients, corporations and communities have?

Organizations spend enormous efforts on keeping up with donor requirements, yet treat today's volunteer as no different from volunteers in the past. It's assumed that today's volunteers think and act as their parents and grandparents did. But our world is a far cry from where it was 30, or even 20 years ago and volunteers have changed right along with it.

Let's recall just a few of the societal shifts in the past years. The Civil Rights movement, the Women's movement, the rise of technology and social media, the rise of a youth-oriented culture, the embracing of self-improvement, the transparency of lives, global shrinking and instant information all have had a tremendous impact on modern society.

People are diverse and evolving. They share feelings and experiences through social media. They seek self-improvement and are less afraid to ask for the things they want. They are keenly aware of the world around them. They feel the power of collective interest and opinion. They get immediate answers to questions and can sift through multiple sources to find the information they seek. "I'll get back to you on this question," is the opposite of the instant answers they find on the internet. Attention spans have shrunk.

Step 2 is understanding the modern volunteer. Who is the modern volunteer and how are they different from volunteers of the past? What qualities and traits do modern volunteers exhibit? How do we engage modern volunteers?

Typically, volunteer studies center on generational differences from the WWII or greatest generation down through the baby boomers, Gen X and Y and the growing influential millennials.

We study the characteristics of each generation, hoping to craft recruitment strategies and retention ploys in attempts to appeal to each one. But is this too simplistic and do we set ourselves up for disappointment when these narrow strategies don't work?

I'm not saying taking the characteristics of generations into account is unwise; I'm suggesting that relying solely on one set of characteristics misses the point: What about the senior who loves technology and has a twitter account while writing her blog on the myths of growing old? What about the millennial who loves mid-century design and wants to live a more simplistic life away from the constant bombardment of online friends?

And what about culture? Can we embrace diversity by simply studying cultural norms? Are we delusional when we declare we are inclusive and appear woefully desperate to prove ourselves worthy of diverse help?

When we, volunteer managers stop beating ourselves up for our inability to mold slick messages that will hook every person in a category and instead, concentrate on our abilities and vast experiences to guide us, then we can center our recruitment outreach on the needs of today's unique volunteers.

There are no perfect recruitment strategies that will hook everyone and no foolproof retention methods that will keep everyone. So, who is the volunteer of the future and if we can't bundle them into convenient groups, how do we redefine their role?

Today's volunteers come from all generations, all cultures and backgrounds and they are embracing the collective changes shaping our world today. They are at least familiar with social media; they have less time to spend, desire flexibility, want episodic experiences, and crave meaning and transparency. They want more control over their volunteer experience.

But many tenets remain the same. Volunteers want meaningful recognition and respect and given opportunities embracing their skills and passions. They want to feel a part of the mission and connect to staff and other volunteers. They want to contribute something tangible and they do not want to waste their time.

And yet, there are some very new components shared by many volunteers today. Volunteers may wish to enhance their resume, learn translatable skills and use virtual opportunities. Unlike their counterparts in years past, they may also wonder what volunteering can do for them versus only thinking of what they can do by volunteering.

These modern volunteers read about scandals in both the business and nonprofit worlds and they desire organizational transparency and want to see solutions to the problems we profess to work on.

Today's volunteers are less inclined to look for solutions to societal problems within organizations burdened by layers of bureaucracy than in years past. They expect charities to work on community challenges instead of serving their own need for growth. Volunteers want to see nonprofits work together for the good of the communities they serve.

We used to worry about volunteers sharing a negative experience with their friends and neighbors. Today we must worry about a volunteer sharing a negative experience with a thousand friends on social media. And share, they will. We are in an age of openness and scrutiny. Gone are the days when an organization could tell the volunteers to "not worry about where donations go."

Today's volunteer expects to be an equal partner with access to organizational goals, priorities, financial dealings and positions on other world challenges. Volunteers may want to know a healthcare charity's stance on hunger or an elder affairs entity's contributions to elementary education. They are keen observers and they scrutinize resource allocation and any partnerships an organization might forge with politicians and/or corporations.

Today's volunteers will not tolerate greed. This non-tolerance extends beyond spending donations unwisely; it also extends to hoarding volunteers and resources.

Volunteers want the reassurance their actions have made a positive impact on the mission and have moved the organization closer to solving societal challenges. The organization that does not recognize this basic tenet will lose volunteers quickly. The new volunteer does not want to dress up and sit at a yearly social function. They do not want cute gifts in the mail or bric-a-brac to put on their shelves.

They do not want the same volunteer of the year offerings that have defined volunteer appreciation for so long. They expect us to tell them the specific impact their time and efforts produce. They want an accounting for their actions. They want professional recognition.

Today's volunteers will 'dabble' and try out volunteering at various organizations. The stigma surrounding quitting jobs, relationships and volunteer roles has faded, so volunteers won't think twice about leaving an organization. Fit is no longer only about whether the volunteer fits the organization, it's now also about whether the organization fits the volunteer.

And what will the future of volunteering look like? Unless we adapt, it may look like a **volunteer block chain**. People who see their neighbors suffering in real time are acting outside the centralization of non-profit affiliation.

Natural disasters and the media coverage of citizen helpers may yield a clue. After hurricanes devastated areas in the United States, droves of citizens with boats, trucks and supplies mobilized to help those impacted by hurricane losses. They were not part of any formal organization. Some banded together through social media. They arrived at the scene of the disaster, went to work and accomplished exactly what they had set out to do. There was no formal application. No interview or placement. No reviewing of policies and procedures. No boundaries placed on them. No waiting for the word "go" from higher ups. No waiting on resources or managers to orchestrate their every move.

These citizen helpers experienced raw, unfiltered volunteering. If volunteer management does not move forward, the future of volunteering will decentralize outside our scope. And this citizen helper phenomena extends beyond natural disasters. What about the citizen who walks by a homeless veteran on the way to work?

The citizen sees this veteran day after day and thinks, "Why is no one addressing this problem," when there are multiple organizations dedicated to helping homeless veterans in the area. This citizen helper may think back to news stories of non-profits who mishandled donations and grumble about ineffective organizations. He may take matters into his own hands, to start a campaign, stage a publicity stunt or raise funds.

And even if this person knows there are multiple agencies dedicated to serving the homeless population, he may think, "Obviously, these organizations aren't solving anything. I see the evidence of it right here every day."

If volunteer organizations do not show **volunteering results**, the citizen helper will assume they can do a better job on their own. They will mobilize without us.

We could see pods of volunteers organically coming together to meet challenges and bypass traditional organizations. We are already seeing corporations put significant resources behind CSR (**corporate social responsibility**) programs in terms of money and employee volunteering. If volunteer organizations don't adapt to the changing landscape, we could be left behind.

Step 2 is redefining volunteers with new terminology. We must show our organizations that not all volunteers are alike and they are not interchangeable. We must rethink how we present our volunteers and how we can reframe the perceptions surrounding them. Along with creating a better understanding of these new volunteers comes an understanding of how the new volunteers think and what they want and need.

The first and critical action necessary is to create a professional terminology to lift up volunteer status and contributions. Words mean something. Words are the fundamental way in which we communicate with one another. Terminology connects concepts which forms impressions or perceptions in the listener.

Take computer terminology for instance. There is an entire vocabulary designed to identify systems and components. It is the way a programmer understands exact meanings. Imagine if a computer programmer wanted to communicate with another computer programmer and said, "I'm working in a high-level language." The term high-level language is broad and really more a category which includes the computer languages C++, Java and Pascal to name a few. Saying, "I'm working in C++" is specific and therefore, understood.

The word 'volunteer' is broadly defined as a person who enters into service. The term is more correctly a category under which there are many types of volunteers. The word volunteer has also taken on this secondary meaning: A person who is selfless and willing. But unfortunately, over the years, it has also taken on certain connotations devaluing our volunteers' contributions.

Connotations surrounding the word volunteer include the notion that volunteers are unskilled, all the same, willing to do whatever we ask and expendable. We rarely associate the word 'volunteer' with professionalism, or leadership or independent. And too often we associate a volunteer with how they are used for a single task and not with their potential. Non-profits aren't looking at volunteers' needs nor their input. Volunteers are figuratively kept in a tightly sealed perception box.

There have been a few attempts to rebrand volunteers by calling them time donors or time givers or skillanthropists. While these terms are nice, they don't capture the essence of all a volunteer offers. And if we wish to elevate volunteers, we must apply terms carrying weight. Clever does not help us anymore.

Terms borrowed from professional languages will elicit an enhanced perception of our volunteers. Let's look at terminology and how to frame volunteers in a more professional light.

Step 2 is redefining volunteers in terms befitting their value.

Volunteer Investor: Do volunteers punch a clock, give a few hours a week and completely forget about us the rest of the time? Of course not. Our volunteers invest so much more in our organizations than just the hours we record. Yes, they invest their time; but they also invest their skills, energies, passions, resources, money, marketing savvy and their desire to see us succeed.

Their belief in our work creates a mindset, one in which our missions reside, ready to be called up when an opportunity to help comes up. It is this extra effort that makes them investors.

They are investing in our missions every time they recruit their friends as volunteers, every time they extoll our services to potential clients and every time they seek in-kind donations from businesses they frequent. They are our everyday ambassadors who pound the pavement looking to help us in any way they can.

Step 2 is making others understand the depth to which our volunteers invest in us. We must illustrate the extra efforts from our volunteers. A way to capture the under-reported activities is by creating a survey asking volunteers to chronicle their extracurricular efforts, something we will explore further.

We must change the perception. Refer to volunteers as investing in the organization by saying, "our volunteers are invested in helping us accomplish our mission. Let me show you the impressive ways they are investing, even when they are not formally recording their hours."

Volunteer consultant: There are countless volunteers who offer their professional expertise. Consultants are people who share paid advice and expertise in a field in which they have vast experience and knowledge. Volunteers who offer their professional skill sets have a unique niche. Refer to these volunteers who share skills and offer advice as volunteer consultants.

Talk about the accomplishments of these volunteers and the incredible opportunity your organization has in accepting these services for free. Calculate how much it would cost to retain the services of a consultant who has similar qualifications. You can say, "We are so fortunate to have a volunteer consultant, Emmie, a practicing attorney with policy review experience who is willing to give of her time to help us review our procedures. The money we save will be substantial and can be put to use elsewhere."

Volunteer talent: When we lump all volunteers into the general term 'volunteer,' we dilute the meaning. The word sinks to its lowest common denominator. Use every opportunity to talk about volunteer talents.

For example, when introducing a new volunteer, refer to the skills and talents she brings. Instead of introducing a volunteer with, "We have a new volunteer, Sela, who is a retired social worker," expound on her talents with, "We have a new volunteer, Sela, who has 20 years' experience working with at risk youth. She knows firsthand the challenges we deal with every day and has been instrumental in program development."

Let's move away from using the general term "volunteer" and redefine volunteers by more specific categories that identify the mission area in which the volunteer participates. Using categories helps to identify volunteers as skilled partners versus the pervasive perception that volunteers are just interchangeable warm bodies meant to fill any simple task. Instead of saying in reply to a request for an event volunteer, "I'll call my volunteers," say, "I will call the event specialist volunteers and I assure you that all of them possess the talents you need."

Volunteer talent pool implies a source of skilled people with desirable abilities. When asked to supply a volunteer for a specific request or task, reply with, "I will refer to my talent pool of volunteers to match one of our skilled volunteers with your request." This is a two pronged approach. It lays a foundation highlighting volunteers' specialized skills and sends the message that not all volunteers want or are appropriate for every request.

Volunteer capital: Volunteers are human capital. They have proficiency in the skills we need and have the desire to see our missions succeed. We can no longer base their organizational value on the outdated notion they are tools to use in whatever ways an organization deems necessary.

Volunteer capital implies a valuable addition of talent, knowledge and skills. Use this term when speaking of volunteers as a whole. For example, say, "this month, our volunteer capital has increased by 5% with the addition of a volunteer consultant and 3 freelance volunteers." It is a subtle term that packs a powerful message: Volunteers bring skills.

Volunteer acquisition: Acquisition is a term implying the attaining of an asset. It is a word that carries weight because the implication suggests the asset is desirable and valuable. You can also preface the term and say **volunteer capital acquisition** or **volunteer skill acquisition** or **volunteer talent acquisition**. Use this term when speaking of recruitment strategies such as, "To increase our volunteer talent acquisition, I am conducting a mini-training session at the Chamber this month. I'm hoping to add additional volunteer talent."

Freelance or pro bono volunteer: Look at the rise of websites geared towards freelance work. Workers are moving away from allegiance to one company and instead, are using their skills for a wider variety of employment. We need to move away from the erroneous concept that volunteers, once they sign on, will not only stay with our organization no matter what, but will happily arrange their time and schedules to fit our needs. Increasingly, volunteers are not willing nor able to commit to a set schedule and instead want to offer us freelance work.

One of the most antiquated volunteer management beliefs is once a volunteer comes onboard, they will stay indefinitely. This notion burdens too many volunteer coordinators with trying to keep a volunteer ad infinitum and causes them to feel the twinge of failure when a volunteer leaves, no matter whether the volunteer moved or retired. The idea that volunteers are to be retained at all costs is archaic and we must lead our organizations away from this outdated and dangerous concept.

The danger in keeping all volunteers perpetuates the stereotype that all volunteers are alike, meaning they are good-hearted, willing individuals that can't hurt anyone. We must educate organizations on the complexity of our volunteer talent pool and not be afraid to admit that some people are not appropriate. Assure staff and management that you, the leader of the **volunteer engagement initiative** are hyper aware of inappropriate volunteers and you will take the steps necessary to keep your volunteer engagement program free from risk.

Speak about volunteers as freelancers or as offering pro bono work. The terms freelance and pro bono support the more correct reality that volunteers are not only in charge of their own timeframe, but will also be in charge of their volunteer experience through the skills they offer. Episodic volunteers are good examples of freelancers as are student volunteers. It is imperative our organizations accept the reality that modern volunteers are less likely to commit to a timeframe dictated by us.

Volunteer talent churn: It's time to stop ignoring the immense role our organizations play in keeping volunteers. It's time to quit sweeping poor treatment of volunteers under the rug. We lose volunteers when a department doesn't use their talents. We lose volunteers when they receive confusing or impossible instructions. We lose volunteers when they are repeatedly ignored. We lose volunteers when they are not offered a position in a timely manner. It's time to point to a poor experience if a poor experience is the reason volunteers leave.

Refer to losing volunteers as the **volunteer talent churn** because the term aptly describes the continuous volunteer recruitment to replace volunteers lost. Without pointing fingers, make it known that keeping volunteers engaged is everyone's responsibility. Offer to conduct classes on working with volunteers. Use this term when explaining the need for meaningful volunteer roles.

Step 2 is identifying and tracking **volunteer recruitment and retention influencers.** Keep track of the volunteers who quit and why they quit by conducting exit interviews. Don't be afraid to share those statistics in a solution-oriented manner rather than as a complaint.

Influencing factors that are out of our control must be identified to accurately evaluate recruitment and retention. Speak to the volunteer talent churn when explaining statistics involving volunteers who leave.

You can say, "We also had three volunteers leave us this month. Two of them said in an exit interview, 'we called several times to get a time to come in and start, but we didn't hear back so we left.' I am trying to convince them to do something else, but in the meantime, I'm also trying to recruit their replacements so we don't continue this **volunteer talent churn**."

We can't fix the problems we keep hidden. We need not be accusatory, but we can point out the reasons volunteers leave to pave the way for improvement.

Volunteer recruitment or **retention influencers**: What distinct characteristics about your organization attracts volunteers? Is it because of organizational reputation, word of mouth, nice facility to work in and mission goals? What are the reasons volunteers give for staying? Do these reasons include meaningful work or friendly staff or flexible hours? These are the positive influencers and on the flip side, there are negative influencers driving volunteers away such as not enough work to do, or being forgotten, or ignored.

By speaking of these influencers in concrete terms, we underscore the importance of everyone's role in keeping influencers positive. You can speak of the influencers at a staff meeting and point out their importance by sharing volunteer feedback. Obviously, you want to hype the positive influencers and call out names of staff who go above and beyond to keep good volunteers.

When discussing negative influencers, remember to frame the negativity in a solution based manner. For example, if volunteers quit because work in a certain department is boring, offer solutions that counteract the negative influencer. Say something like, "Our skilled volunteers are looking for more meaty assignments, but they are willing to devote an hour of their time to filing, instead of taking four-hour shifts." Staff will perceive the volunteer manager who always offers solutions as a leader, not a complainer. And change is more effective when you ease your organization into a **mediated change** instead of simply saying, "Our volunteers refuse to do this job anymore."

Volunteer track: We know each volunteer is unique. They come to us with unique abilities, individual ideas of what volunteering means to them, their own spin on how much time they want to spend, and how consistent they wish to be. But again, lumping all volunteers under one big tent makes it appear all volunteers are clones of one another and volunteer management is nothing more than making a few pleasant phone calls before one willing volunteer says "yes."

Step 2 is slotting our volunteers into categories or tracks. Categorizing helps our organizations understand we cannot just pull volunteers out of the big volunteer hat.

For instance, place one-time volunteers on the episodic track because they cannot be counted on for recurring roles. As a solution-oriented volunteer manager, always offer the assurance you are continually recruiting volunteers to move from one track to another.

This is an example of **internal recruitment**, a term we will explore further in Step 4. Other track designations include a student track where volunteers engage in service learning and gain resume enhancing experiences. Service learning volunteers require a more nuanced volunteer experience that matches their reasons for volunteering. There are also ambassador tracks, client service tracks, office specialist tracks, event specialist tracks, etc.

Some volunteers will cross over and become floaters which generates another track. But if your volunteers need additional training to move into a new track, pencil them in as future volunteers, pending their additional training. Penciling them in reinforces the importance of training and dispels two myths: The first is untrained volunteers can do no real harm and the second is there's no work involved in readying a volunteer for service.

Tracks are a visual that partitions volunteers into realistic numbers. In the past, if you had 100 volunteers on a list and someone requested a volunteer for an assignment, they assumed you had 100 people to draw from.

Volunteer tracks show the actual number of volunteers you can draw from for each assignment. If your organization covers a wide area, then add geographic regions to tracks to further illustrate the challenges facing you when placing volunteers.

One ancient, yet pervasive volunteer management misnomer is that a volunteer manager's job is to "talk volunteers into taking assignments." Tracking volunteers not only helps frame the availability of volunteer talent, it also gives visual evidence of the challenge in recruiting a volunteer to travel a distance to fill an assignment outside his geographic region.

If your tracks show there are substantially more volunteers signed up for one particular area, you can show the correlation between volunteers' enthusiasm and the types of roles they want. As for the sparsely populated tracks? Show the reasons the volunteers aren't interested in doing those tasks. Maybe the tasks require too much responsibility or are too time consuming or there's too much extra training involved which makes these reasons **retention influencers**.

The more evidence we have that shows volunteer preference, the more likely we can advocate for roles our volunteers favor and on the flip side, the more evidence we point to showing volunteer disinterest in certain tasks, the more we can lobby for those tasks to change.

Step 2 is reframing volunteer contributions to reflect all the volunteer extras. As investors, volunteers contribute so much more than the hours we record. Although some of their contributions verge on intangible, it is up to us to capture more than traditional hours so we can illustrate the enormous impact volunteers have on our organizations.

Look for more than the volunteer hours you are currently recording. Think about all the ways in which your volunteers add value beyond fulfilling tasks. It is in these areas that volunteers truly invest in our missions and further our goals. There are many additional areas not typically represented by reports. A few areas are:

- Spreading the word about your organization's good work. Volunteers will talk, which makes them **organic ambassadors.** They spread messages about our organizations all over town, to their friends, their gym buddies, their neighbors, the appliance repair guy, and the man at the post office who needs your organization's services.

Are the messages our volunteers spread factual? Volunteers will talk and it is up to us to make sure they have correct information. Are volunteers equipped with the same verbiage and tools as the marketing staff? Refer to your volunteers as **WOMM** (word of mouth marketing) **ambassadors.**

Equip them with verbiage cheat sheets, business cards, and direct access to intake. Direct access closes the loop on volunteers having to report potential clients to the volunteer manager who will in turn contact the appropriate department.

The more direct route a volunteer can take to elicit help for potential clients means precious time will not pass before they are able to refer someone. Jumping through too many hoops will cause volunteers to put off referrals or forget to report them. We need to give our volunteers a direct pipeline to our intake departments.

Lobby for the tools your volunteers need to speak to potential clients. Most volunteers are more comfortable speaking on organizational behalf when we encourage them to be spokespersons. Help senior management see there is a potential small army of WOMM ambassadors just waiting to be trained.

Let's just ask this question: How influential are the WOMM ambassadors? Ask one of your volunteers to identify their **circle of influence** (people they come in contact with during say, a month-this includes their fellow worshipers, club attendees, neighbors, friends, doctor's office personnel, etc.). Multiply the number of people in that circle by the number of your volunteers. Now there's a lot of influence going to waste. Present a graph showing the huge potential outreach program within your volunteer talent pool.

Let's say one volunteer identifies over 200 people in their circle of influence. Multiply that number by 50 volunteers and you now have 10,000 people in your volunteers' circles of influence. Isn't this an impressive number? Investing in our volunteers as spokespersons is a cost effective marketing method waiting to be unleashed.

- There's another area that is typically not recognized as part of volunteer contributions and it is procuring in-kind donations. Volunteers typically are involved in many community areas and have a wide array of contacts. Share an organizational wish list with every volunteer and give them the contact information for the in-kind donation specialist so they can contact the specialist directly when they find someone willing to donate an item.

- Many fund raising experts write extensively about how to convert volunteers into donors, as if volunteers were a new, untapped resource, but volunteer managers know volunteers do not need converting. They already donate.

These 'volunteers as donors' articles illustrate the disconnection between organizational perception of volunteers and reality. Organizations that don't know about and don't acknowledge donations from volunteers are short-sighted.

Volunteers' monetary gifts need special recognition and organizations should use this information when soliciting donations from others. Encourage your organization to publicize the impressive fact: "75% of our volunteers give money regularly." This statement packs a powerful message. Volunteers are **transparency meters**.

Volunteers are widely perceived as good people who give of their time to make the world a better place and will leave an organization that is not ethical. They know organizations from the inside, can see firsthand the work being done and if they give money, then potential donors will infer that the organization is transparent and spends money and resources wisely. Once again, volunteers are a valuable asset beyond the hours we typically record.

Volunteers want to be included in donation campaigns as a courtesy rather than as a bid to squeeze more money from them. They deserve a special packet acknowledging their volunteer status, so depending upon your database, there needs to be a cross-referencing to identify volunteers as contributors of both time and money.

On the flip side, organizations should encourage donors to volunteer. We know that organizational fund raisers pay attention to marketing advice and marketing experts stress using stories to appeal to donors. So, why not suggest that donors immerse themselves in the heartwarming stories by experiencing the work firsthand? What a great way for donors to connect with the mission.

Organize a **donor day** and treat them to an inside view. Allow them to shadow a volunteer while they are interacting with clients and families or doing other tasks that further the mission. What if, after an inspiring day volunteering, these highly regarded donors had great things to say about the volunteers and your initiative? Think about their circle of influence and the deserved good PR you would receive. Offer to conduct a special orientation for donors.

Surveys are handy tools you can tailor to gather useful information. Use them to support a hypothesis about your volunteers or to bolster a theory you have developed. Spend some quality time developing surveys. Surveys can do double and triple duty so you're not sending a survey every time you have a question or thought. Add survey questions to volunteer sign-in sheets and capture data every time a volunteer is present.

Let's look at sample questions on a survey combining capturing data on two important volunteer areas: The extra work volunteers engage in for the mission and the intrinsic benefits volunteers receive from volunteering.

- How often do you speak to others about our organization? What do you tell them?

- Do you search for in-kind donations? If we supplied you a list of the items we currently need would you feel comfortable asking your friends or the businesses you frequent for a donation?
- Do you recommend our services? How do you refer someone? What do you tell a potential client?
- How do you recruit other volunteers? What do you tell them?
- Do you recommend us as donation recipients to your church, club, etc.?
- Do you feel empowered to speak on our behalf? What do you need to feel empowered?
- How many hours per week or month do you feel you spend working to further our mission outside of your regular volunteering duties? This includes recruiting other volunteers, asking for donations, explaining services, etc.
- What has volunteering meant for you? How has it enhanced your life? Did you: a-learn a new skill, b-begin a new career, c-enjoyed the camaraderie of other volunteers, d-other.

Based on the survey results, lobby for specialized training for your volunteers by your marketing and fundraising departments. Encourage the departments to write into their budgets an allocation of supplies needed (business cards, cheat sheets) so your volunteers confidently continue their ancillary work. Use a sign-in sheet to record the extra hours.

Showing how volunteers bring new talents, skills and perspectives will encourage looking at volunteers in a new light. Call these volunteer contributions **volunteer fresh**. Are the members of senior management aware that volunteers who work in the corporate world have access to expensive training and the latest business trends?

Volunteers who continue to work, or have recently retired, or are active in an area of interest are a wealth of desirable knowledge. They are the equivalent of sending staff members to costly business seminars.

Volunteer fresh means opening the organization's doors to free up-to-date ideas and methods. Ask your volunteers to author a presentation based on their specialized knowledge and encourage your CEO to partake in the fresh perspectives of your volunteers.

Organizations cannot hire an infinite number of skilled staff and most overlook the deep talent pool of volunteers. Continually remind upper management you have access to sources of knowledge and skill. Refer to your **volunteer talent pool** or **volunteer skill pool** and look for ways to offer volunteers' fresh voices in areas such as planning and development, finance, grant writing, marketing, and human resources.

Create bios on your volunteers. Start with the volunteers who have the most requested skills and gradually add more volunteer bios as staff becomes accustomed to referring to the talent pool. Again, call these volunteers "pro bono," or "consultants" to increase their status.

Add volunteer photos to their volunteering "resumes" and post in a shared area. The more staff see volunteer skills, the more likely they will think of asking for volunteer help when working on projects. Seeing volunteer skill potential will ignite staff's creativity and spur them to think in possibilities.

Step 2 is integrating volunteers into the mission. Refer to volunteer engagement as **Mission Centric Volunteer Engagement.** As you work towards helping your organization understand the modern volunteer, how they think and what they contribute, add in the needs of these modern volunteers and the ways to keep them coming back.

Integrating volunteers into the mission includes recognizing volunteers have their own unique mission view. Many volunteers offer their services because your organization helped them and because of their experience, they want to give back and support the next person.

These volunteers have a deep understanding of the services your organization offers. Their personal connection fuels their desire to further the mission and are a wealth of positive, usable information.

Because their experience is personal, they can give vital in-depth feedback on how staff and volunteers treated them, what worked or didn't, etc. Many organizations send out surveys after a client has been a recipient of services. But surveys are skewed. Imagine if your organization could sit down with a recipient of services and pick their brain.

They can, because volunteers who have received services have those thoughts to share. Encourage your organization to tap into the experiences of these **mission experienced volunteers** to better understand and improve organizational processes. Put together a **mission experienced volunteer focus group** to offer constructive feedback.

Today's volunteers don't view themselves as subordinate to the program but rather as a partner in its success. So, instead of conducting yearly performance reviews, ask volunteers to share accomplishments and goals with you. By sharing their perspectives, you gain an understanding of the mission areas volunteers deem most important. If no volunteer says, "I'm proud I tri-folded over a thousand letters for a mail campaign," then perhaps folding letters doesn't rank high on the volunteers' list of meaningful work.

The more volunteers rank their accomplishments, the more a pattern will emerge. What roles give them the highest sense of accomplishment? What roles give them the opportunity to feel part of mission excellence?

The emerging patterns can serve as a guide for creating new volunteer roles, which serves for better recruitment and retention strategies. Patterns can also help you lobby to remove less meaningful volunteer roles and instead, relegate the less desirable roles to an "only on occasion" status.

Volunteer goals can be instructional in much the same way. Ask volunteers to set **mission centric goals** for themselves. What would they like to accomplish moving forward? What do they see as their primary mission? What direction do they see the organization going in and how do they anticipate getting there?

Planning with the modern volunteer instead of planning for them sends the message they are an integral part of the organization and are instrumental in accomplishing mission goals. One area volunteers frequently cite for the reason they connect with an organization is the knowledge they are a vital team member.

Often organizations overlook volunteers and forget to include them in messaging, perks, opportunities and marketing. It may not be intentional, but the lack of inclusion sends a message as loud as if the organization had stated, "volunteers are not on the same par as the rest of us. They are separate. We like them, but we don't consider them integral." Remind your organization to think of volunteers as contributing investors in the mission.

And what about the all-important volunteer recognition? How does the modern volunteer view it? Do they want more luncheons? Do they seek more awards? Do they care at all about balloons and cake?

While the status quo presents volunteer appreciation as an event (noun), it is time to modernize our ideas of volunteer recognition and reframe it more as a verb (appreciate), one that must be an ingrained part of non-profit culture.

Step 2 is reframing volunteer appreciation. It is time to rethink volunteer appreciation and move towards referring to volunteer recognition as **Volunteer Value Recognition** or **Volunteer Value Acknowledgement**. This is a pivotal shift in recognizing volunteers. Instead of recognizing them for *being volunteers,* we are now asking to recognize the *contributions volunteers are making* and the significant impact their actions have made on the people we serve.

It is a subtle, but profound shift. Reduce outdated words from recognition, ones describing volunteers in personal ways, such as "tireless," "heartfelt," and "giving nature." These adjectives emphasize the volunteers' selfless nature, something ingrained into organizational psyche. We know volunteers are nice. We know they are selfless and giving and are heartfelt.

We need to move towards emphasizing the more powerful **impact verbs** which speak to how volunteers changed, improved and helped the mission. Use **results-oriented** or **impact-oriented** examples when speaking about volunteer accomplishments and contributions.

Tell staff how crucial it is for them to be a part of this **value recognition** and **acknowledgement** and explain how this helps stave off the **volunteer talent churn**. Help staff relearn appreciation by equipping them with ways to endorse volunteer work. A few ways to do this are:

Construct a handy drop box so staff can record positive stories of volunteer engagement. Share these stories with volunteers. Refer to the stories at staff meetings as examples of effective volunteer appreciation. Reiterate the value recognition.

Conduct "how did we do" surveys by calling clients who received volunteer help. Ask questions about the volunteer's impact such as, "tell me about the things you could do or accomplish because of volunteer help."

Reframe these stories into a **volunteer impact report** and illustrate the direct impact such as "because our 20 volunteers advocated for 32 clients in our court system, all 32 received satisfactory outcomes. And here are testimonials from actual clients about the impact our volunteers had on their lives."

Visit key staff quarterly to gather testimonials on volunteer value and share with volunteers through an email blitz, newsletter, etc. Continuous positive feedback is a no cost volunteer retention method. These meetings can also intercept any brewing problems or questions staff may have concerning the volunteers they work with.

Sift these conversations into concrete stats by asking staff pointed and measurable questions like "what have you been able to accomplish, take on, or improve with volunteer help?" The concrete stats then become part of your **volunteer impact report**.

Make a repository for volunteers to share their experiences. These stories most always are examples of mission impact. Encourage volunteers to include stories other than direct client contact.

Instances such as encouraging a total stranger to contact the organization for help shows WOMM impact. Examples of volunteers reaching out to local businesses to donate goods or services shows **resource procurement impact**. Share these stories and keep statistics for year-end reports.

Step 2 is redefining the volunteer role and implementing the strategies to serve their needs. Volunteers often site comprehensive volunteer training as a reason they stay with an organization. Training is a critical investment in your volunteers. From the moment they say yes, we must train them to succeed and continue to educate them on policies, updates and goals.

Training is a three-step process. Training in three steps ensure volunteers are prepared to contribute and feel a valued member of the team. The three steps include:

- Orientation.
- Onboarding.
- Continuing Education or the Re-recruitment of Existing Volunteers.

Orientation is more than an introduction to your organization. It is the bond connecting a new volunteer to mission work. It is an extension of recruitment strategies and the place to showcase heartwarming stories, testimonials and calls to action. Orientation answers volunteer questions such as, "What difference will I make," and "what will I get from volunteering?" It cements the feeling that a volunteer has made the right choice by attending your orientation.

Onboarding is the hands-on training which integrates volunteers into their role. Staff or experienced volunteers can train a new volunteer and introduce them to their duties. A volunteer handbook is an essential tool that lays out policies, procedures and helpful information.

Some volunteers will require more in-depth onboarding if they work with clients or have complicated duties. The more upfront work we put into our volunteers by meaningful onboarding, the less chance mishaps will occur.

Continued education is actually a process in re-recruiting existing volunteers. It says to them, "We want to keep you informed and educated so you stay." Education can take many forms, from volunteers attending a staff seminar on the latest mission information to creating a volunteer speaker bureau in which volunteers share their expertise with one another. Newsletters are great ways to share updates and spark renewed interest in the mission.

Step 2 is redefining the volunteer role and recognizing volunteers need a streamlined process to volunteer. Often you hear we should make volunteering easier. Perhaps easier is the wrong word. Practicing risk management keeps us from having a volunteer program where "anything goes." There are policies, procedures, background screening, training and follow-up for this reason: Protecting our clients.

But, although making it easier is not exactly the right word, we do need to streamline our process. Nothing is more aggravating than hearing about an urgent need for volunteers and then, when trying to volunteer, not hearing back from us. It frustrates potential volunteers when they are left hanging.

Think of the ways a potential volunteer contacts you. Can they call? Do they answer an ad on a volunteer search engine? Do they drop in? Is there an email option through your website? Do they tell staff or other volunteers and then you find notes left all over your desk?

Step 2 is creating a working system for the modern volunteer. It doesn't matter if you use digital folders or physical binders, or an expensive database; we must contact potential volunteers within 24 hours of their inquiry during the work week. Invite them to the next training or open house. Ask them to come in for an interview. Leave them a message or an email.

Above all, make volunteers know you want them. Words matter. What is the first impression you give a potential volunteer? Do they hear busyness in your voice? Do they hear phrases like, "you can come if you want," or "I think we might have an upcoming training, let me check?"

Most volunteer managers are swamped with work. We will talk more about delegation in Step 4, but here is a prime example of the need to delegate. Reaching out to prospective volunteers is a perfect job for existing volunteers. And it doesn't have to be the same volunteer every day.

Write a script for a volunteer to use when calling prospective volunteers. Craft an email template to send to potential volunteers. Put together a distribution list so you can group potential volunteers into a mass email. Ask for a stand-alone email address which serves potential volunteers, something like volunteernow@myorganization. Ask for permission for the volunteers who help you to have access to the volunteer email. Then, their ability to focus on keeping potential volunteers informed and in the loop will pay off greatly for you, the overly busy volunteer manager.

I had three or four volunteers helping me, and they kept binders of potential volunteers. They would call, send flyers and schedules of trainings and open houses, and follow-up consistently.

I remember potential volunteers telling me on many occasions that we were the only organization that actually answered and got back with them. This happened thanks to the volunteers who took control of engaging all prospective volunteers.

Another area that needs streamlining is the volunteer application. If it is outdated, then potential volunteers will view your organization as out of touch. Look at your application and see how it stacks up to the needs of the modern volunteer. Does it seem authoritarian? Does it appear to place volunteers in a box? Does it include a section dedicated to creativity, leadership or growth?

Think of your application as a marketing tool, another invitation to join your organization. Ask questions capturing your volunteers' potential. Are they future leaders? Can they help solve challenges? Will they feel empowered? Look for skills and talents to include in your talent pool and your volunteer bios.

Speak about **recruiting for volunteer potential** or **recruiting for volunteer talent**. Don't be afraid to be selective in onboarding volunteers. Do not hesitate to explain not all volunteers will fit, and not all volunteers are appropriate for **mission centric volunteer engagement.** Stand firm knowing you are making every effort to ensure your volunteer team consists of competent and vetted volunteers. Speak to quality over quantity and point to the responsibility you have to provide the best to clients.

One way to reinforce your commitment to providing quality volunteers is to review the number of incident reports involving a volunteer. An incident report typically occurs when a client or family member reports a misstep. Staff may have spoken to them in an inappropriate manner. More serious incident reports may accuse staff of stealing or happens when a client trips over organizational equipment.

If the amount of times your volunteers are reported for a misdeed is low, use these statistics to emphasize your meticulous attention to vetting and placing volunteers. Point to your comprehensive training in preparing volunteers to represent your organization in a safe and appropriate manner. Firmly reiterate you will provide clients with only appropriate volunteers and you will not compromise to fill tasks with warm bodies.

Step 2 is redefining the volunteer role to elevate contributions by the modern volunteer. It is a huge undertaking and is not an overnight change. Educating your organization and guiding them into looking at volunteers in modern, improved ways will take persistence and strength.

When you see a positive shift in the way your organization views volunteers, it will take a modern leader, one ready to implement step 3.

Step 2 Checklist:
- ✓ Understand changes in modern volunteers
- ✓ Redefine volunteers with new terminology
- ✓ Redefine volunteers in terms befitting their value
- ✓ Define the many ways in which our volunteers are invested
- ✓ Identify volunteer recruitment and retention influencers
- ✓ Slot volunteers into tracks
- ✓ Reframe volunteer contributions to reflect volunteer extras
- ✓ Integrate volunteers into the mission
- ✓ Reframe volunteer appreciation
- ✓ Implement strategies to serve modern volunteers' needs
- ✓ Streamline processes
- ✓ Create a working system for the modern volunteer
- ✓ Elevate volunteer contributions beyond hours recorded

Step 3: Redefining the Volunteer Manager Role

Stefan's three volunteers wished him good luck before he headed to the meeting with his executive director. She listened politely as he described the art therapy project his volunteers had spent weeks developing. He ran down the carefully thought out plan and pointed to the volunteers' passion and enthusiasm. He presented a commitment statement signed by each one of the project volunteers.

His executive director nodded her head. Stefan finished his presentation by saying, "Our volunteers want to make a difference and they're prepared to put the work into this."

The executive director smiled an end to his talk. "Well, thank you for bringing this to me today, Stefan. I will think about what you said. In the meantime, what are your plans for the volunteer luncheon this year?"

Herding cats. Coordinating senior citizens. Planning tea parties. Scheduling thank you events. Blowing up balloons. Chatting with volunteers. Having fun. Are these the perceptions we, volunteer managers give people? And how do these perceptions fit in with leading the new volunteer, the changes in volunteer management and **mission centric volunteer engagement**?

Volunteer coordinators' roles have traditionally existed to fill requests from upper management and key departments and to provide volunteer help when called upon. Management also expected the volunteer coordinator to record volunteer hours and recruit volunteers by giving talks at women's clubs or by sitting at volunteer fairs. Coordinators were supposed to on-board volunteers and stop them from doing harm. They were viewed as cheerfully persuading volunteers to take on any task, no matter how mundane or uninspiring. Coordinators were thought of as ancillary staff.

Organizations expected volunteer coordinators to support the directives from senior management and to provide volunteers without questioning the assignment, methods or appropriateness. Volunteer coordinators were considered support staff. They existed solely in a reactive model.

Organizational senior management did not encourage the volunteer coordinator to question volunteer roles or take part in planning volunteer engagement. They never expected volunteer coordinators to complain about conditions either for the volunteers or for themselves.

Most times, organizations lumped the volunteer coordinator under the secretarial umbrella as there was no comparable category in which to place them, especially when determining salary. The problem was, if organizations deemed volunteer coordinators managers, then salary would have to reflect managerial status.

Non-profit senior management did not include volunteer coordinators, and did not groom them for leadership roles, even though volunteer coordinators managed more human capital than most all other organizational staff.

Because they were in a supporting role, the volunteer coordinator was not included in management or leadership training. There was no credit given for engaging diverse groups of unpaid people. Coordinating volunteers was a 9-5 position, although volunteer coordinators routinely filled in for absent volunteers, fielded questions and solved problems whenever needed. Volunteer coordinators worked more than a 40-hour week and yet, were not acknowledged nor compensated for the extra hours.

Few considered engaging volunteers a particularly skilled job since volunteers were perceived as willing, obedient souls who desired nothing more than to please their chosen organizations. How easy it was, organizations surmised, to ask them to complete a task. There was little understanding of the work involved in readying a volunteer to serve mission goals. The coordinator label meant easily executed duties.

Organizations lumped all volunteers into the same bland basket and expected volunteer coordinators to give equal attention to every person who expressed a passing interest in the organization. Seldom was there talk of the nuanced talents required to mediate inappropriate behavior, to direct the misguided volunteer or to develop integrated volunteers.

Recognition was not given for the upfront efforts to bring out a volunteer's best or help them invest in the mission. And if a volunteer caused problems, fingers pointed at the volunteer coordinator, as if she was negligent in training the wholesome, good-hearted volunteer. Organizations perceived volunteers as good, committed people who just needed a phone call to spring into action.

I remember my first interview for a volunteer coordinator job. My future boss asked me if I got along well with senior citizens. I assured her I did. In those days, the predominant sought after skill for a volunteer coordinator position was the ability to be nice. Nice people made great volunteer coordinators because niceness was what it took to convince a volunteer on a Saturday morning to drive 20 miles to retrieve the important paperwork a staff member forgot to pick up.

Volunteer coordinators were often isolated and could only find one another through local volunteer coordinator groups. More often than not, volunteer coordinator group members were too busy to attend meetings and there was never enough money to afford leadership training. These volunteer coordinator groups commiserated with one another, but, being islands onto themselves, knew of no emerging trends within their own areas or countries, much less the world.

And then came the internet. Volunteer coordinators found one another. They found expert help. They realized their complaints were universal, others shared their concerns, their intuition was correct and there was a systemic devaluing of volunteers and volunteer professionals. They found a voice.

Today, we refer to volunteer coordinators as volunteer managers. The more appropriate title is "leaders of volunteers" or "leaders of volunteer engagement," which better describes the complex nature involved in recruiting, training, placing and keeping volunteers.

Today's volunteer manager needs to be a polymath (Greek: having learned much). A polymath is a person versed in a variety of subjects. Today's leader of volunteers has to juggle diverse skills.

But let's stop here for a moment and examine this widely accepted concept. For most volunteer managers, the variety of skills used to engage volunteers is a source of pride. In the past, volunteer coordinators described their jobs as being "a jack of all trades," or "wearing many hats."

The problem with those flippant descriptions is a jack of all trades is considered a master of none. Perpetuating the assumption that we, **volunteer engagement professionals** run around in chaos, switching from one skill to another destroys our credibility as professionals and *paints engaging volunteers as a series of **unrelated tasks**.*

We cheer on volunteer Edward and then run off to counsel volunteer Sophie. We look at volunteer Azmir's vacation photos and then make a few phone calls. When we talk about our skills as though they are unrelated, we give the impression we bustle about like people who have no relevant skillset. We must stop this perception and instead, classify our talents as interdependent entities working together to achieve an outcome.

Volunteer engagement requires sharply defined, complimentary people skills. Let's visualize our skills as part of a wardrobe. Each skill is a shirt or pair of slacks or jacket. When getting dressed for the day, we pair a shirt with coordinating slacks, shoes, jacket, and other accessories.

Pieces work together, whether for a formal, business or casual outfit. Our closets contain wardrobes, not random pieces of clothing we wear one at a time.

Volunteer management skills are very much like a wardrobe. Volunteer engagement skills complement one another and we wear them for specific purposes. Mediation means we are using skills to bring people together for a greater purpose. Recruitment means we are using skills to inspire and engage. Retention means we use every skill we have.

The volunteer manager must be an exceptional negotiator, a deft motivator, thoughtful mediator and an accomplished communicator. Today's volunteer manager must excel at communicating a vision, be a master of intuition and active listening, and be able to pair volunteers with assignments sure to inspire them. Today's volunteer manager must exemplify the very best in leadership.

Step 3 is redefining our skill set. It's not like we are fixing a leaky pipe and then sitting down to write a song. Our skills have a singular purpose and directly relate to each other. We use them to recruit and retain good volunteers. We need to get away from spreading the misnomer that we are "masters of none" and move toward connecting the skills we use in the term, **volunteer engagement skills.**

Volunteer engagement skills also encompass leading volunteer teams. There is a tremendous difference between teams made of staff and teams of volunteers. Teams made of staff are **established teams** while teams of volunteers are often **fluid teams**. Established teams take less ongoing leadership than fluid teams. Fluid teams need much more from their leader.

Established teams:
- Practice together to find workable rhythms.
- Are familiar with one another's needs.
- Have systems in place.

Fluid teams:
- Work in the moment.
- Must get to know one another quickly.
- Must innovate instantaneous workable methods to accomplish goals.

Volunteer engagement professionals work with both established and fluid volunteer teams (think volunteers gathered at an event or corporate volunteer groups). Leading a fluid volunteer team takes agile leadership skills, including:

•Ability to convey and continually bring the team back to the big picture, also known as **mission centric inspiration.** Volunteers working with other volunteers and staff they do not know well need a reason to do the work. They don't have familiarity and the "I've got your back" camaraderie found in established teams.

Volunteer engagement professionals must be nimble in forging a **camaraderie of mission inspiration** to get the best from each member. Mission goals must be communicated continuously for this fluid team to work well together.

•Ability to establish a cocoon of trust among team members. Fluid team members don't know one another well and it is up to the volunteer engagement professional to set a tone of inclusion and acceptance. Each member must understand their contributions are valuable and their concerns are heard.

•Ability to skip mentoring steps and still reap productive benefits. Established teams take time and mentoring so they work well together. Fluid teams do not have time to work out their interconnected rhythms and it is up to the volunteer engagement professional to identify volunteer team members' strengths and shortcomings. A fluid team's success depends on the leader's ability to piece the team together for maximum productivity.

To explain fluid teams, ask a senior manager to imagine switching out members of her team on a daily basis. How would her leadership duties change and increase? How would she establish trust and convey mission importance? How quickly would the team be able to get the work done? Point out that fluid volunteer teams require continuous agile leadership to achieve maximum results.

The modern volunteer needs a competent leader, one who is forward thinking, able to discern the volunteer's needs and able to advocate for conditions favorable to volunteerism. It takes developed volunteer engagement skills to recruit, inspire, match and keep good volunteers.

Step 3 is redefining the volunteer manager role. As volunteer managers redefine the modern volunteer as volunteer investors and highlight the enormous contributions they make, then along with this new normal is the necessity to redefine the person responsible for their engagement. A modern volunteer needs a modern leader to succeed. It is time to stop ignoring the volunteer manager's role in developing volunteers.

Examine the reasons you are a volunteer manager. Step back and look at it with clear vision. What are you passionate about? Seeing volunteers get excited about volunteering? Seeing clients get the intimate and personal help only a volunteer can give? Witnessing the best in volunteering? These passions give us job satisfaction. They are what we get up for and cling to after a long, hard day.

Sometimes however, when we cling to our passions, we tune out all the other parts and pieces that make up our jobs. We can become frustrated with anyone or anything not supporting the passionate lens through which we see our volunteers and their contributions. This frustration can cripple us as leaders.

Step 3 is expanding your passion and dedication. Take the passion you feel for volunteering and break the wall separating you from professionalizing your department. Expand your passions to include purposefully elevating your volunteer engagement initiative.

Being concerned with professionalizing the volunteer engagement program does not mean losing all the intangible goodness volunteers bring. It does not mean selling out to corporate ways. It means connecting the soul to the brain.

It means dedicating yourself to creating an exemplary program, one in which intangible goodness will be more respected, more valued and more in demand. By devoting your time to uplifting your volunteer initiative, you are laying the foundation for even more volunteer success.

It's akin to building a sailboat. When we passionately weave the sails and revel in the beauty of our sails unfurling in the wind, but skimp on the craftsmanship when creating the hull, the boat will sink. The hull of volunteer programs need the same dedication and passion as we put into watching the beautiful sails against the blue sky.

As the new leader of volunteers, appreciate the beauty of a strong, supportive foundation. It will give you the support you need to see your passions grow.

Immediately discard the word "coordinate" even if it is in your job title. Remember your complimentary engagement skills and use the term, "**engagement**," when working with volunteers as in, "I'm working on engaging our volunteer Sam right now, be with you in just a moment." You are not coordinating (placing or arranging). You are engaging (attracting and securing).

Coordinating implies there is little effort involved in placing a volunteer. Coordinating implies volunteers come willingly and stay indefinitely. They engage themselves and it is the volunteer coordinator's job to ask for help, then issue directions.

Engaging speaks to the hard work involved in attracting and keeping volunteers. Its broad scope gathers the myriad of challenges facing volunteer managers. It encompasses tasks such as motivating, smoothing rough patches, counseling, matching, providing additional training, bolstering, reassuring and other deeply profound people skills that all work in tandem to engage volunteers. It is volunteer engagement.

Step 3 is engaging in improved recruitment. Adding **volunteer talent** is essential to forming a productive volunteer team and the modern leader of volunteer engagement uses marketing wisely.

Recruitment is no longer a hastily worded ad collecting dust while sitting on the shelves of your local publications and the e-sites advertising volunteer jobs. The new volunteer manager understands recruitment ads must do more than describe a bland job, like "event volunteers wanted."

Forgo the broad, simplistic titles like "caring hearts needed," or "hold a hand." Write targeted ads which speak to the importance of the work. Design ads in three ways:
- Description of job.
- Benefit to client and organization.
- Benefit to volunteer.

Instead of using the outdated "caring volunteers wanted for meal delivery to homebound seniors," reframe the ad to appeal to potential volunteers and their desire for meaningful work.

Use dynamic ads, such as ones issuing a challenge: "Homebound seniors suffer from isolation. Will you help?" Use statistics such as "three of five seniors are not receiving proper nutrition. We need your help to fix this."

Or use a real story: "Harvey's best friend is his volunteer, Chet. Other Harvey's are waiting for their best friend. Please join us."

Experiment with ads. Track which work and which don't. Ask prospective volunteers how they heard about you. Get rid of ho hum language and revamp your ads to convey excitement, fun, a sense of wonderment and warmth. Above all, convey meaning.

Step 3 is recognizing what modern volunteers want and moving towards those goals. Remember, modern volunteers don't want traditional volunteer appreciation in step 2? Volunteer appreciation for the modern volunteer means an action, not an event. They want to be shown the results of the time they spend with us.

Does this mean we have to do away with luncheons and awards altogether or do they have a purpose? Awards are beneficial if their emphasis serves a volunteer sustainability goal.

Instead of trying to choose one volunteer worthy of an award, give awards that convey an **impact message**. Award groups of volunteers and volunteer initiatives that illustrate volunteer value and contributions. This doesn't mean we have to get clinical and ignore our volunteers' giving spirits. It means incorporating the caring nature of volunteers into the larger picture; the results of their caring nature.

Point to cooperation and team effort by volunteers. In place of awards for hours spent by one volunteer, weave in the strategies and methods groups of volunteers used to accomplish goals. Use the verbiage from your **volunteer impact report** and tie the award to furthering the mission.

If your organization's mission goal is to "eliminate hunger and food insecurity," give awards tied into the mission statement. One example would be an award for "Increasing Food Insecurity Awareness."

The award would go to all 15 volunteers who spent 125 hours conducting 12 food drives and engaging 15 businesses in the area. When you present the award is the proper time to point to the volunteers' collective determination and giving spirit.

Another mission award, the "Eliminating Hunger Award" would go to the volunteers who kept the food bank open. When presenting this award, cite the number of people impacted by the volunteers' actions, again borrowing from your impact report.

Step 3 is broadening our volunteer training concept. As we saw in step 2, meaningful orientation, onboarding and continued training is crucial to sustaining volunteers. But we can add a bonus volunteer integration element into the mix by involving staff in our volunteer education plan.

One way to give overworked staff an opportunity to renew enthusiasm is to suggest each staff member take a turn and teach a segment of volunteer orientation. Experiencing the awe and excitement through the eyes of new volunteers will help reinvigorate their original passion for their work.

This practice has dual benefits: Volunteers feel they are important team members while staff gets to better know and understand the volunteers they will work with or encounter. It may be difficult to carve out the time needed for busy staff to teach volunteer orientation in person, so an option is videotaping staff members giving tips or pointers, explaining their jobs, sharing stories and expressing encouragement.

Even if staff cannot spare the time to teach in person or on video, there is one thing we can do to strengthen staff's buy-in. We can ask staff for their input into the subjects and areas they would like us to cover during volunteer orientation, onboarding and continued educational training sessions.

Enlist staff in preparing a **volunteer education topics list** by asking staff these questions:

•What is the most important thing volunteers should know before they get started?

•What volunteer behaviors do you wish we addressed prior to their volunteering? Please site examples.

•How can we prepare volunteers for the future? What areas need reinforcing or updating?

•What do volunteers need to know in order to work in my area and be effective?

•Why is my work critical to the organization? How can we impart the necessity of this work to volunteers?

Keeping staff in the continuing education loop means they will be part of volunteer integration and therefore be more accepting of volunteers because they have had a hand in preparing volunteers to become part of the team. Bringing staff and volunteers together for a higher purpose is a step in establishing yourself as a leader.

Step 3 is reframing your title. Refer to yourself as a **leader of volunteer engagement**. Volunteer coordinators have always been humble souls who stood in the shadows, preferring to let their volunteers shine, an attribute while admirable, will not help further volunteer engagement.

Being a strong leader is not the same as being an egotistical leader and on the flip side being a humble leader does not equate with weakness. A strong, humble leader focuses on the strength of the work and the merits of the team, not on themselves.

A strong, humble leader extolls the accomplishments of his/her team. A strong, humble leader advocates tirelessly for the needs of the team. A strong, humble leader inspires everyone around them. You can be a strong, humble leader of volunteers.

If calling yourself a **leader of volunteer engagement** still seems self-serving, then use the verb, lead. Say, "I'm here to lead volunteer engagement," or "My job is to lead the volunteers." Using the verb puts the emphasis on the work rather than the person. Once the verb "lead" becomes ingrained, then add leader when referring to yourself.

Step 3 is explaining your work. Explain that volunteers, as **investors** or **consultants** or whichever term you are using, are **account holders** and hold a **volunteer account** in your organization. Explain that the leader of volunteers is equivalent to an **account manager** and is responsible for maintaining these accounts. Let's again borrow terms from other professional entities and apply them to volunteer engagement.

Volunteer Account: Each volunteer invests in our organization. They invest as currency, their time, efforts, skills, passion, knowledge, hope for a better world, personalities, talents, and reputations. As the manager of these volunteer accounts, it is the **volunteer account manager's** responsibility to make certain the account holder is engaged and wants to continue investing.

While each investor is unique, there are certain universal tenets affecting volunteer investors in either a positive or negative way. Take a moment and outline what you believe these tenets to be. They may include:

- Recognition of impact: How does the organization recognize volunteer impact? Remember, step 2 and the discussion of **value acknowledgement** and **value recognition**? How is my organization sharing impact with this volunteer investor?

Investment firms share the statistics on investor capital and how it is growing and what the prospect for the future holds. Investors expect to see their investments being handled with care or they will take their capital elsewhere.

How do organizations show volunteers the return on their investments? Volunteer account managers can show organizations how to report investments to volunteers.

A report containing only volunteer hours served is like a bank informing you that you deposited x amount of currency. The information is obvious.

Bank account holders want to know how their bank is using capital and how their money is growing. Volunteer investors need to know how their **volunteering capital** grew.

They will question whether their **organic ambassador** activities made a difference. Does it matter that they spoke to their homeowner's association about the mission? Did it make any difference that they procured a donation? We need to show them that every investment they are making is paying off to meet mission goals and strengthen the organization's standing in the community.

Formulate an **impact report** which outlines the **ROI** (return on investment) for your volunteers with detailed information outlining the impact volunteers have had on the mission. How were clients impacted? How did donations or awareness increase? How was staff able to accomplish more?

- Personal Development: How does the organization invest in the volunteers' personal growth? Continual training is essential. Just as banks educate their investors on how to grow their capital, organizations can educate volunteers on how to grow their investment of time and skills by continuing to educate them on mission-related areas.

Does the organization offer ways to develop leadership skills or wellbeing? Ask to include volunteers in any educational offerings focusing on subjects related to mission performance and personal improvement. Management may agree to include volunteers in one portion of a leadership seminar.

•Integration into Team: How does the organization make volunteers understand they are important members of the team striving towards one shared goal? Are volunteers excluded from events? Are volunteers given a separate lounge area? Are they given a separate section of the newsletter? Are volunteers referenced in presentations and speeches on an equal par with staff? Point out any disparities and lobby to include volunteers in press releases, reports, marketing information and staff recognition. Explain that volunteer investors need visuals to keep investing.

Step 3 is showcasing volunteer uniqueness which requires a skilled leader of volunteers to find and keep volunteers engaged. It means showing the fine points of your work.

Key Volunteer Account: No two volunteers are alike. The 80/20 rule states 80% of effect comes from 20% of causes. You can apply this to the explanation of key volunteer accounts.

Explain that 80% of volunteering comes from about 20% of active volunteers. In addition, to keep key volunteers who are producing 80% of the work, you must spend quality time engaging them.

This means for one time volunteers, and episodic groups who may come and go, the responsibility for managing them must also include the department or staff member utilizing them and not relegated to you, the leader of volunteer engagement.

Assure everyone that you will give episodic volunteers every courtesy, but you will not direct them, get them snacks or entertain them without the involvement of the department benefiting from the help.

Your responsibility is to follow-up and invite them to further their volunteering, but the direction they receive on the day they volunteer will be shared with staff overseeing the activity.

Put together a "working with volunteers 101 course" for staff who will oversee episodic volunteers and offer it throughout the year. The point here is twofold:

- To move staff towards taking responsibility for engaging volunteers and not leaving it solely to you, the volunteer manager who has bigger picture responsibilities.
- To instill a realization that volunteers have levels of commitment and that your time cannot be divided ad infinitum. You must spend your time wisely by engaging key volunteers who contribute.

As a volunteer manager cultivating key volunteer accounts, explain that your job is to cultivate existing key accounts and develop new key accounts. **Key volunteers** are any volunteers you consider indispensable.

These volunteers may be the ones who say yes at the last minute, are dependable week in and week out, give the most hours, recruit other volunteers, help manage groups of volunteers, and are exceptional at the tough assignments or anything else you consider crucial.

They are the ones who seek donations, always attend meetings and look for additional ways to help. Their solid investment in your organization makes them a priority and you must spend quality time cultivating their involvement. They are your leaders, potential future staff members and arbiters of sound ideas.

Your other responsibility is to develop new **key volunteer accounts**. That entails encouraging volunteers with potential to invest more deeply in your organization.

It means mentoring potential key volunteers and attending to their needs in the same way banks court potential key customers. Potential key volunteers need encouragement, an understanding of their worth and their concerns addressed for them to invest more deeply in our missions.

Volunteer project management is a term correctly describing what a volunteer manager actually manages. We can slot most volunteer tasks into a project mode, including the recurring ones. Speak of managing volunteer projects and engaging volunteers as complimentary skills. The two skill sets intersect to provide volunteer value and impact.

Remember our wardrobe and all the varied skills that combine to present a well-dressed volunteer engagement professional? Volunteer managers also accessorize themselves with project management skills used to make projects run smoothly.

Project management requires skills such as risk management, organization, team leadership and problem solving. While volunteer engagement requires emotional intelligence and soft skills, including inspirational communication, balancing, and persuasion techniques, project management requires the hard or technical skills such as reporting results, measuring impact and extensive planning.

Volunteer managers are known for their soft skills. To professionalize ourselves and our departments, we need to focus on developing and showcasing our technical skills.

But let's stop here for a moment. So far, we've outlined the volunteer manager's role from a perspective meant to uplift volunteer engagement.

Every time we elevate our volunteers, we organically pave the way to elevating the volunteer manager role. After all, a modern volunteer needs an adept volunteer manager.

Step 3 is viewing the volunteer manager role from another perspective. Let's switch views and look at elevating the volunteer manager role from the organizational perspective. How does an organization view the volunteer manager role when understanding the new volunteer? Will staff and administration naturally realize a vibrant volunteer initiative that attracts quality volunteers will need an exceptional volunteer manager or must we show them?

This may sound crazy, but we, volunteer managers have to forge a little separation from the organization. Isn't that counter intuitive? Aren't we supposed to be team players? How can separating ourselves from our organizations help?

Well, let's ask two questions. Are the volunteers a product? Is the volunteer manager a product manager?

Wait, again. People aren't products, they're people. And we continuously fight against the notion that volunteers are faceless tools. Volunteers are not like a product, such as athletic shoes, where each shoe comes out of the assembly line exactly the same.

But yet, cleaning services, limo services, in-home nursing, babysitting and even celebrities are products composed of people. People products are about selling personalities, talents, skills, hard work and dedication. Sounds a lot like volunteers, doesn't it?

We can't balance fighting against thinking of volunteers as tools while calling volunteers products, but what we can do is to refer to them as volunteer assets or talents.

And this is where separation from the organization comes into play. As a **volunteer asset or talent manager**, the leader of volunteers develops the ideal asset (volunteer) for the customer (the organization).

The whole product idea, which we are terming volunteer asset or talent focuses on the volunteer manager's skillful input. No longer are we allowing organizations to picture volunteers as people who do not require any volunteer manager involvement.

The shift here is to remake yourself as an entrepreneur who is in charge of a people asset, one you develop, engage and cultivate to further mission goals. Your experience and knowledge coupled with your training, coaching, mentoring and extensive efforts in getting to know volunteers make up volunteer development. It is critical to volunteer success.

And what are your responsibilities from an organizational standpoint as this **volunteer asset manager**? It is to develop, provide and adjust.

Step 3 is embracing two interconnecting entities: The volunteers and the needs of the mission. There are two perspectives to consider and each perspective means viewing your job with different lenses.

One lens looks at the volunteers, their needs and wants (volunteer engagement). The other lens looks at what the volunteer asset can accomplish to help the organization further its goals (volunteer impact).

Neither lens is rose-colored but rather, they are practical lenses that when used together give the modern volunteer manager a tool in which to see the direction providing the highest engagement and the most impact.

Let's imagine looking at the volunteers through a yellow lens. We see what volunteers need to succeed. Then we look at the volunteers through a blue lens. We see what will further the organization's mission. When we can see the volunteers through a combination of the two lenses (green), then we have achieved a balance.

Step 3 is develop, provide and adjust. Our first responsibility as a **volunteer asset manager** is to develop volunteers. Speak in terms of **volunteer talent or skill development**.

Great volunteers do not fall out of the sky. Explain that your training, mentoring and coaching along with in-depth interviewing, monitoring and guidance develops volunteers equipped to fill mission centric tasks.

Lead senior management into understanding you are continually developing volunteers to provide a volunteer asset or talent designed to further the mission. Developing volunteers takes work.

Think about it this way: Would an organization ask a brand new staff member to go into the home of a client on his first day? Of course not. Organizations are very careful to train and mentor new staff members before expecting them to do their jobs and it should be no different with volunteers.

Developing volunteers also means you are guiding and coaching volunteers to ward off problems before they start. The more we educate volunteers on how to work with staff and clients, the fewer headaches we will have down the road.

Staff and upper management have little understanding of this very important volunteer engagement step. They rarely realize all the work that goes into preparing a volunteer to work within organizational systems, to adhere to organizational expectations and to support, not hinder hard-working staff members.

List the areas your volunteer development includes, such as:
- Thoroughly briefing volunteers on mission history and goals.
- Immersing volunteers into organizational culture.
- Preparing volunteers to work with vulnerable clients.
- Preparing volunteers to work alongside staff in cooperative ways.
- Educating volunteers on their rights and responsibilities.
- Integrating volunteers into specialized areas and tasks.
- Reviewing policies and procedures.

Because volunteers are not prepared to come in off the street and produce, we need to talk about volunteers in a **developmental stage**. Volunteers may first undergo training or mentoring or they may be involved in an experimental program.

The point is, a portion of the volunteer asset is not ready for rollout, because warm bodies cannot provide proper services to vulnerable populations or are prepared to produce desired results.

For years, organizations expected volunteer coordinators to assign volunteers to tasks without understanding the efforts it took to prepare a volunteer. Volunteer development received little attention which fostered the notion that "once someone signs up, you have a ready to go volunteer."

By looking at volunteers as a human capital asset, we can understand there is no magic involved in readying a volunteer for service. On the contrary, volunteer assets involve research, strategy and extensive development.

Once your volunteer asset completes the development stage through your onboarding process and training, then you can provide the volunteers to achieve a goal, fill a task, further the mission or pilot an initiative. Knowing the needs of your customer (organization) is key to developing and providing volunteers. Look at requests from the customer's perspective (remember the blue lens above).

Companies who produce products listen to their customers' desires so they can offer the products consumers want. By tuning into the needs behind volunteer requests, we can understand how to better provide volunteers we have developed.

Does this mean we must fulfill every request? Of course not. If customers tell a company they want flying shoes, the company will say, "Flying shoes are not possible, at least at this moment." As entrepreneurs and volunteer asset managers, it is no different when organizations request a volunteer for a task difficult to fill.

We may not have a "developed" volunteer for every task. Volunteers may not have the skills that fit the task. They may not have the temperament necessary for a fit. Speak about developing volunteers' skills, attitudes and understanding of mission goals.

Voice your pursuit to provide **quality volunteers,** i.e., the ones who are not a risk management nightmare, are not lone wolves doing whatever they want, are not unnecessarily taking up staff time and are not harming the people we serve.

On the flip side, companies look to develop products that consumers don't know they want or need. In this same vein, volunteer managers can strategically offer a volunteer asset which furthers the mission in ways staff and senior management have not thought of nor realized was possible.

Offering new avenues for volunteers to further mission goals is one innovative way to show leadership. Champion a project that engages volunteer talent in ways not thought of before. Solve challenges with your volunteer talent and highlight new avenues of furthering the mission.

Adjusting through feedback is the third stage of volunteer asset management. Feedback comes from the organization, from clients and from volunteers.

It is this critical feedback helping us adjust to strategically develop and provide engaged volunteers equipped for mission roles. When fielding comments or critiques, be sure to acknowledge the feedback and use it later to support your adjustments.

For example, if a staff member tells you he spends a lot of time showing volunteers where the restroom, break room and lounge are located, use the feedback to improve development and refer to it when placing new volunteers.

Say, "I heard your comments and now, in orientation, I walk the volunteers through the office and point out the restroom, break room and lounge. I have also created a "welcome to the team" sheet highlighting the information they need to get started. This will help free up more of your time due to the time I spend in developing our volunteers to succeed on day one."

Step 3 is recognizing the need for agility. The **agile leader of volunteers** recognizes the fluidity in volunteerism. Agile is a term applied to project management. It implies that the agile leader possesses an ability to bend, to adapt, to change and to evolve according to results and challenges.

Remind your organization that volunteer engagement must embrace agility, especially when beginning a new volunteer venture. Should a directive come down from upper management and you have not had a hand in the planning, be clear about the necessity of being agile, as the volunteers will have input, questions, barriers and challenges in meeting the goals. It will take time and extensive effort on your part to manage the back-and-forth adjustments needed to help volunteers get on board.

Your role as the leader of volunteers is not to coordinate volunteers in a new venture, but to successfully engage them in cooperative ways. Again, it takes effort.

Agility means that volunteer involvement does not come from a top down approach, but is forged from a cooperative partnership between management and volunteers that allows for adjustment. Agility takes into account volunteer needs and guarantees success.

Explain that for any volunteer project to succeed, the ability to adjust to challenges and barriers is essential. **Agile projects** plan for bumps, are flexible enough to shift when necessary and can pivot during trying times. Keep a project worksheet and record any challenges impeding progress. Offer flex solutions to address these challenges to not only make the project succeed, but to harness the best of your volunteers and keep them engaged.

Speak in terms of agile leadership and agile initiatives. We know the agile leader recognizes fluidity. But an agile leader also balances the ability to encourage successful traditional thought while disrupting the status quo. How does the **agile leader of volunteers** accomplish this? By incorporating these aspects:

- Respect and inclusion: Agile leaders work within the system rather than from the outside. They engage all stakeholders in the change process rather than excluding their input. This means allowing staff and/or volunteers who are resistant to change a forum in which to give their opinions. It means connecting stakeholders to the bigger picture: Mission goals.
- Clarity: Agile leaders are clear about mission related direction and not afraid to be honest. Being open and honest about mistakes or shortcomings means being vocal about the willingness to work to fix them. Consistent messaging is key: We are here to provide the best for the people we serve.
- Instilling trust: This means maintaining a professional approach and not allowing personal feelings to disrupt the process. It means following through on promises. The only promises you can guarantee are the ones promising doing your best, following up and keeping an open mind. It only takes a few broken promises to lose volunteer trust.

Step 3 is modeling organic leadership as the basis of volunteer management and encouraging its practices. Most volunteer managers excel at **organic leadership** in their volunteer programs. Organic leadership is almost a paradox. It champions leading by not leading.

It is the antithesis of the top down structure most organizations operate under. In most organizational structures, directives come from senior management. Volunteer managers work on filling the tasks outlined in the directives. But here is where the top down structure ends.

Volunteer managers do not give top down directives to their volunteers. Instead, they collaborate with volunteers to find the ways to fill tasks while structuring the task parameters to satisfy the volunteer (remember the yellow lens above). The volunteer services department is an organic structure within the top down organizational model.

The new leader of volunteer engagement encourages the adoption of organic leadership by modeling its successes to senior management. Showcase projects executed by volunteers. Explain the organic methods used to arrive at project success such as agile planning, collaboration with motivated volunteers, trial-and-error testing, re-evaluation and modification.

Remind senior management that volunteer feedback with adjustments is crucial to volunteer results. Point to increased volunteer satisfaction from volunteers who participate in collaborative initiatives. Share ways you think organic leadership can work in other organizational areas.

Step 3 is planning for mission centric volunteer engagement. It is the goal of the new leader of volunteers. Advocate for a seat at the planning table. You may have to prove yourself first and one way to do so is to put your ear to the wall and listen for any discussions of organizational challenges or goals. Formulate how volunteers can be helpful in attaining these goals or meeting these challenges.

Put together a proposal of how to involve volunteers and submit it to senior management. It can be as simple as offering volunteer help to call clients on Friday afternoons so that problems are intercepted before the weekend, thus alleviating on-call staff from making multiple field visits. Emphasize that you are always creating mission centric roles for your volunteers and then lobby for a seat at planning meetings, reiterating that the more you are privy to challenges, the more you can help.

Step 3 is developing your personal brand. The new leader of volunteers is his/her stand-alone brand. As an agile, strong leader, you are the face of your department. What will people see as you walk towards them? Will they see a dedicated, fair, solution minded individual who is a champion of results? Will they want to work with you?

As your own brand, you have control over the impression you give. Remember, in the pre-step, disrupting ourselves? Our efforts to reframe volunteer management must include reframing the way we are viewed.

Offices are mini ecosystems full of personalities and emotions. Do you engage in office gossip? Or do you excuse yourself and stay out of the emotional traps? Do you hold grudges against snarky co-workers?

Or do you calmly keep them at a professional arm's length and realize their behavior is a reflection on them and not you? Do you get into it with passive aggressive staff?

Or do you realize their game only works if they can snare you into taking part, so you ignore the emotions they want you to feel? Do you let opinionated volunteers manipulate you? Or do you hold your ground and explain the policies and procedures in place in a calm, but firm manner?

Being known as a **solution-oriented** or **results-oriented leader** means having no time for emotional anchors. Ignore the emotional traps some staff and volunteers lay for you and stick to logical, professional thinking. Clarity of thought helps us to examine situations and arrive at logical conclusions.

Take time before replying to emotionally charged messages. Remember, passive aggressive criticisms are about getting you to play the game rather than about actual events. There is nothing wrong with challenging passive aggressive commentators by taking a solution or results-oriented approach.

If a staff member complains, "I never get any volunteers when I want them," reply with this carefully worded question: "Can you please give me examples of the times you could not get a volunteer?" Follow this question with, "I'm asking so I can fix the barriers we have to making sure you get the volunteer help you require. I want to make sure you get results."

If a staff member says, "thanks for sending me volunteer Jackie. She was a handful," reply with "I'm hearing a challenge with our volunteer Jackie. Please give me concrete examples of why you considered her a handful. This way, I can counsel her for future assignments. I want to find a workable solution."

As your own professional brand, offer your skills in other organizational areas. Offer to develop motivational stories for marketing in the community. Offer to teach other staff how to manage projects. Offer your skills as a speaker to represent your organization at your local community college. Offer to share a satisfaction survey for staff.

Show your skills off and elevate your personal brand. Every time you boost your contributions, you elevate the volunteers and the volunteer initiative. The more you showcase your **organic leadership**, the more you will be able to shape your role.

Step 3 is redefining the volunteer manager role by advocating for resources. Along with explaining the modern volunteer, their contributions and needs, you are also introducing yourself as their capable leader. This is the time to advocate for resources.

Make a wish list of the resources you feel will help you better engage your volunteers. Assign priorities to them. Choose one important resource, one which is doable and present it to senior management.

Show why this resource is important, why it will further the mission and why it will be a **return on investment** (ROI). Explain a positive cause and effect, such as "investing in educating volunteers will prepare them to better serve our clients and advance our mission goals."

Be prepared to stay the course and every time this resource could have been put to use, diplomatically remind senior management how it would have helped. Ask for a grant written to obtain this resource. Then, when you institute this first resource, it is crucial to keep statistics on how this resource benefited the organization.

For example, if you ask for money to send volunteers to a seminar, *track the increased participation and increased skill set* of the volunteers who attended. Record testimonials from staff, clients and community that show increased satisfaction by the volunteers who attended the seminar.

Use these testimonials and statistics to support the next request for resources. Ask a key volunteer to gather your stats.

The new leader of volunteers makes strategic budget decisions and prioritizes recruitment and retention, but if no budget is allocated for volunteer services, then it is time to request one.

Give your administration several categories in which a budget will increase the effectiveness of volunteer contributions. These categories include volunteer recognition, volunteer tracking software, marketing, outreach and training. Be prepared to keep statistics on ROI.

Step 3 is championing partnerships. Organizational departments are more than "customers" utilizing our volunteer assets. They have services that can help us. By internal partnering with your marketing department, clinical staff, finance, and support services, you remove the "us vs. them" mentality that can plague volunteer managers. Seek to establish symbiotic relationships with staff. How can you help them and in return, how can they help you? Some simple ways include:

- Marketing: Send a volunteer out with marketing personnel on speaking engagements. This ambassador volunteer can handle anything from greeting and handing out brochures to speaking about the volunteer experience.

In return, ask marketing to help you craft recruitment ads, or improve the volunteer section of the website. Explain that volunteer ads also reach potential donors and supporters and therefore, well-designed volunteer ads do double duty.

- Clinical staff: Ask volunteers skilled in healing touch, massage, Reiki or other alternative therapies to take part in a "staff wellness day." In return, ask staff to give mini educational sessions for volunteers who work with clients. Point to the correlation between educated volunteers and better client service.

Partnerships are the cornerstone of buy-in. Give and take breaks the silo mentality that plagues non-profits. Reaching out allows departments to participate in creating volunteer engagement which leads to support for the program.

Partnerships extend far beyond the organizational walls. The modern leader of volunteers will partner with other organizations and corporate groups for maximum community benefits. More on this in Step 5, reframing sustainability.

Redefining the volunteer manager role means becoming a champion of messaging. Advocate for social media accounts so you can craft messages designed to attract and engage your volunteers.

Explain you have the experience and knowledge to build messages resonating with existing volunteers and potential volunteers. But there is also tremendous added benefits in showcasing volunteers and their work. These messages will reach the community, donors and clients.

Emphasize highlighting volunteers in social media for maximum impact. Pointing to volunteer involvement reassures potential clients that a team of highly trained and talented members of their community will be there to assist them and add an extra layer of service.

Engaged volunteers also show potential donors that a thriving fellowship of people are committed to seeing the mission succeed. Witnessing volunteers from the community help an organization reassures potential donors that their money will be well spent.

Volunteers in key positions enhances community pride and motivates fellow citizens to participate in continuing the good work. The cyclical message becomes: The more donors and supporters see the good work being done by volunteers, the more donations and support will pour in.

Step 3 is recognizing emerging trends and capitalizing on them. One growing trend is CSR or **corporate social responsibility**. Businesses are moving towards more engagement with the communities they profit from. Customers tell businesses this is something important to them. Employees want to work for employers who are socially responsible. Voices on social media shame businesses who fail to give back.

Profits are now about more than good products and services. Standing within the community is also important. There is a blending of profit and charity as more businesses are developing a social responsibility wing. What does this mean for the modern volunteer manager? It means your skill set is desired by private companies. Have you thought about working in the business sector? Does this go against your principles? Or do you view this as something organically arising and you may further the idea that everyone is responsible for building sound communities? Can you offer your volunteer management skills to a business looking to improve their CSR?

Embracing CSR is more about creating a partnership than it is about creating a one afternoon activity for corporate volunteers. Study the businesses in your area. Who has shared values or is passionate about your organization's work? Has a business owner availed themselves of your services, but hasn't yet formulated a CSR plan? Can you help them devise a plan, especially if the cause is dear to their heart?

The new leader of volunteer engagement will seek out partners where none previously existed. Perhaps you have a skilled volunteer who can help you develop a CSR plan to present to local businesses. Corporate volunteering can be so much more than sending a few employees to weed the grounds for a photo-op.

A partnership with businesses paves the way to donations, pro bono services and marketing help. Fostering a partnership based on shared values will help establish your credentials as a visionary leader. Your partnership blueprint will be an example to forge other partnerships benefiting both the organization and the corporate partner.

As leaders of modern volunteer engagement programs, we must step out of the shadows and claim our rightful place in non-profit leadership. Think about it this way: Non-profits are formed to meet a challenge.

But why form a non-profit? Why not just go out and work on the challenge? Because there is an underlying reason to form a non-profit. The reason is to gather support, in the form of money, workers, funding, donations and volunteers. As leaders of the largest human capital support, volunteer managers have extensive knowledge and experience to offer non-profits.

We need to realize that by becoming more proactive and visible, we are elevating our initiatives because great programs have great leaders. Be sure to jot down your leadership successes and hang onto the list. We have a use for them in Step 4.

Step 3 is establishing yourself as the leader of volunteer engagement. As you find your voice and become your own brand, then it's time to begin step 4.

Step 3 Checklist:
✓ Redefine your skill set
✓ Redefine the volunteer manager role
✓ Expand passion and dedication
✓ Improve recruitment

- ✓ Embrace what modern volunteers want
- ✓ Broaden volunteer training
- ✓ Reframe your title
- ✓ Explain your job
- ✓ Showcase volunteer uniqueness
- ✓ View your volunteer manager role from the organizational perspective
- ✓ Embrace 2 interconnecting entities: the volunteers and the mission
- ✓ Develop, provide and adjust
- ✓ Recognize the need to be agile
- ✓ Model organic leadership and encourage organizations to adapt
- ✓ Plan for mission centric engagement
- ✓ Be your own brand
- ✓ Advocate for resources
- ✓ Hone partnerships
- ✓ Embrace trends
- ✓ Establish yourself as the leader of volunteer engagement

Step 4: Reframing Priorities and Vision

Suki whispered into the phone, "I'm sorry, can you hold for a moment?" She laid the receiver down on the desk. Her supervisor with arms folded, stood in the office doorway.

"Margaret asked me to come see you," her supervisor said. "She's wondering where you are on getting those volunteers for tomorrow's event. Can you please get back to Margaret? Now? She needs that count."

Suki nodded and as her supervisor walked away, she picked up the phone and said to the person on the other end, "I'm so sorry, but I will have to call you back. I have an emergency to deal with."

In the old volunteer management model, volunteer coordinators' priorities would change hourly as challenges bombarded them from all sides and filled their day with chaos. Upper level management expected a volunteer coordinator to drop everything and fill tasks or solve issues created by the power holders who, most often did not understand leading and engaging volunteers. When favoring one department over another, senior management would cave to the loudest organizational voices demanding service, which would then take precedence over anything a volunteer coordinator was working on, no matter how essential.

Take Suki's experience, for example. Marketing asked her to provide volunteers for an event they opted to attend at the last minute. But unbeknownst to marketing and Suki's supervisor, Suki was on the phone, finalizing an agreement with a local university for student volunteers to complete service learning as a requirement for classes related to her organization's work. She had followed up on a volunteer's suggestion and contacted a professor who believed in hands on learning. She had met with the professor on multiple occasions to firm up a viable plan. Suki's weeks of courting the university would mean, if they agreed, guaranteed volunteer help for years to come.

So, what was her priority in this instance? Dropping everything to procure a few volunteers for a last-minute event or continuing to pursue a sustainable volunteering partnership that might lead to additional resources?

As society evolved, volunteer coordinators struggled to fill archaic tasks while keeping up with the rapidly changing volunteerism landscape. Engaging volunteers became more challenging. Keeping volunteers grew more difficult. Recruiting volunteers to fill the slots vacated by retiring volunteers got harder. Yet, organizations continued to view volunteer engagement in the same, old ways. Volunteer programs devolved into fitting the round, modern volunteer into square, worn-out holes.

"Why can't we get volunteers like we used to?" Non-profit executives weren't listening deeply to their volunteer managers. Overworked staff didn't want to hear how hard the volunteer manager's job was when their jobs were also harder due to societal changes affecting them and the squeeze of doing more with less.

As staff shrunk, the expectations placed on volunteer departments rose. "Let's get volunteers to do it," was heard in boardrooms across the globe as organizations struggled to reduce staff but increase productivity. And so, volunteer coordinators were asked to provide more volunteers for mostly outdated roles while new volunteers rejected the same roles their predecessors had little problem filling.

Let's go back to Suki's situation. Volunteer coordinators have universally had to drop everything to rectify poor planning from organizational staff who expected the volunteer department to pick up the slack. This **reactive priority** setting stopped volunteer coordinators from strategically setting **proactive priorities**. It kept volunteer coordinators on the hamster wheel.

All over the world, organizations remain stuck in linear thinking models. Linear thinking as it applies to volunteers looks like this: Request→Find Volunteer→Volunteer Accepts→New Request.

As Albert Einstein pointed out, "we can't solve problems by using the same kind of thinking we used when we created them." This statement accurately reflects the chasm between volunteer management realities and the status quo.

Every volunteer manager is a wealth of experience and information on engaging volunteers, yet they have minimal input into crafting volunteer roles and their programs' directions.

Organizations continue to view volunteers much like office equipment. They exist for use. However, office equipment is not alive with motivations and needs. And don't forget, enormous potential beyond traditional jobs.

Because engaging volunteers is like no other profession, the people who understand it best must set the priorities. The longer we, volunteer managers try to explain and strategize the changing world of volunteerism without success, the bigger the problems grow.

Then, blame for lack of volunteers is unfairly placed on the volunteer manager who struggles to meet demands. But let's face it. Even the most capable volunteer manager cannot prop up a failed system. It has to change.

In the past, organizational hierarchy relegated volunteer coordinators to ancillary or secondary status. This secondary status increased frustration because volunteer coordinators managed more human capital than staff with higher pay and loftier responsibilities.

Yet, volunteer coordinators committed to the work, and endured the low pay, low status and deaf ears. They realized the intrinsic worth their volunteers brought to not only the mission, but also to themselves.

Volunteer coordinators dreamed of volunteer engagement programs that would catapult their agencies into the future. They craved harnessing volunteer power and unleashing them to solve problems and address challenges. They looked forward to the day when volunteers became vital partners. But linear thinking kept them scrambling to continue operating in a volunteer churning factory.

Step 4 is reframing priorities and vision. As you guide your organization into understanding the modern volunteer and your expanded role as their leader, then to establish a strong volunteer department, take charge of reframing your priorities. And what must the first or top priority be? Furthering mission centric work.

Step 4 is rebranding our volunteers. Bear with me here. Remember in step 3, we asked whether we, volunteer managers are product or asset managers? Because the words product and even asset dehumanizes our volunteers, we need to think of another term that encapsulates all the areas to which volunteers add value. Our volunteers add humanity, caring, fresh ideas, skills, compassion, talent, knowledge, experience, time, advocacy, patience, monitoring and outreach. In simplest terms, we can say our volunteers contribute.

Let's look at ourselves as leaders, not only of volunteer engagement but also of a developed volunteer asset. We are **leaders of volunteer impact**. It's time to prioritize a shifting away from exclusively viewing our jobs as engaging volunteers in tasks. On its own, engaging volunteers implies we spend our day making volunteers feel good so they do our bidding. This notion is wildly inaccurate because it leaves out the critical result of our efforts. We engage volunteers to provide impact.

We must get away from the limiting perception that our function is to sweet-talk volunteers into undertaking chores and move to expand our role in providing volunteer impact. In no way, does this diminish the connection we have with volunteers, nor does it devalue our role in engaging them.

In no way does this ignore their humanity. Rather, it bundles all these lofty ideals and brands them in terms of their importance to reaching organizational goals.

What does any organization offer to the people and community it serves? Support? Help? Resources? Understanding? Avenues? Financial Aid?

Volunteers fit within each one of these offerings. Often, volunteers are the face of each offering. And, to harness the potential of these offerings, (i.e., support, help and resources) we need to bundle the offerings together in a more understandable and identifiable way.

It is difficult trying to make our organizations understand each volunteer contribution separately. By bundling, we can translate all these intangibles into something tangible we can measure, inspect and highlight.

Actually, we already speak in terms of our volunteers as a brand when we talk about their care and compassion, their connection with clients, their donation of money and resources and their organic ambassador activities.

But universally, we have concerned ourselves with redefining our roles to explain volunteer management and how we motivate and engage volunteers from the volunteer standpoint. It's time we embraced the second and equally important part of our jobs. It is time we spin our efforts 180 degrees around by showing volunteer contributions and value to organizational missions.

Step 4 is elevating volunteer impact. It's time to call volunteer managers **leaders of volunteer engagement and impact**. This comprehensive term speaks to the duality of volunteer management: Engaging volunteers and overseeing volunteer contributions. For too long, we have acted as the folks who "get volunteers to do things," which in a warped way only covers volunteer engagement. This singular view of volunteer management does not recognize how engagement and impact exist in a symbiotic relationship.

We must place equal emphasis on volunteer value and the role we play in moving our missions forward. As **leaders of volunteer engagement and impact,** we integrate meaningful volunteer participation with volunteer contributions to the mission in a combined effect which I call **volunteer synergy**.

The combined effect is the ideal result of our efforts. Let's look at the two proficiencies a successful **leader of volunteer engagement and impact** uses and how they mesh for **volunteer synergy**:

- Volunteer satisfaction (volunteer engagement) skills. Volunteers are fully engaged in meaningful work.
- Volunteer contributions (volunteer impact) skills. Volunteers produce results that further goals.
- Volunteer synergy occurs.

Volunteer Managers' Volunteer Satisfaction Skills:

- Interviewing and placement of volunteers to match their passions and talents.
- Introducing pilot projects to harness volunteer creativity.
- Designing roles to engage modern volunteers.
- Training and education designed to prepare volunteers to succeed.
- Advocating to include volunteers in programs, perks and opportunities.
- Mediation and problem solving.
- Continual encouragement and inspirational coaching.

Volunteer Managers' Volunteer Contributions Skills:

- Matching well developed volunteers for mission centric tasks.
- Partnering with organizational departments.
- Relationship management or the cultivation of optimal interactions between volunteers and the organization.
- Ability to accept and use feedback.
- Partnership planning with staff for impactful volunteer roles.
- Training volunteers to tasks and mission purpose.
- Designing forward thinking initiatives.
- Communication for successful project implementation.
- Innovative ideas for volunteer involvement.

Volunteer Synergy:

- Mission centric work-related initiatives and roles for volunteers which satisfies volunteers and furthers the mission.

- Soliciting feedback from volunteers, staff and clients with the intent to use feedback to further program goals.
- Agility in adjusting projects to work.
- Sharing of volunteer contributions with staff, clients, volunteers and the community.
- Creating value added volunteer roles.
- Results-oriented methods.
- Solution-oriented methods.
- Growth-oriented goals.

Step 4 is recognizing the importance of volunteer synergy. It drives a **leader of volunteer engagement and impact** to create a synergized experience. The integrated halves establish the optimal brand (the one that people will picture in their minds when they hear "volunteer department") and consist of images that invoke engaged volunteers doing mission centric work.

Volunteer synergy occurs when we combine our **volunteer engagement skills** with **volunteer impact**. Remember in step 3, looking at volunteers through a yellow lens (engagement) and then a blue lens (mission goals)? Volunteer synergy is the combination of the two lenses. Green occurs when volunteers are fully engaged and satisfied while achieving mission goals.

It is the harmonious balance that both attracts volunteers and changes the world for the better. It is everything you do, from your recruitment ads and volunteer meetings to your mediating difficult circumstances paired with unleashing volunteer skills and potential. It is the recognition that engagement and impact are symbiotic. **Symbiotic volunteer engagement and impact** exponentially enhances, supports and increases each other.

Volunteer synergy is that moment when you peek in on a volunteer hugging a distraught client and you can feel the connection in the room. But make no mistake. You had a hand behind the scenes in developing, encouraging and matching the volunteer who has put their skills to maximum use. It is **mission centric volunteer engagement and impact** in the purest form.

Step 4 is reframing our priorities and vision by adjusting our view of our roles and embracing the enormous impact potential we have on our organizations. As we develop volunteer programs meeting the needs of our volunteers while furthering mission goals and we redefine ourselves as leaders of volunteers, then we can market our "brand" to our organizations. What does this marketing entail?

Let's go back to Step 1, unleashing the will to disrupt. Remember the "**building the future of volunteer engagement project**," and the **"building the future of volunteer engagement project updates**?" It is time to add impact into the initiative and now name it "**building the future of volunteer engagement and impact project**." Marketing the impact portion comes from gathering the statistics you have been capturing through surveys, testimonials and reports and updating your organization on **value added volunteer contributions**. Schedule regular updates on volunteer impact that highlight all the tangible and intangible volunteer contributions.

We can borrow from successful marketing campaigns and market with confidence. Because you are now consistently advertising volunteer value and impact, you can add creativity to your brand. What are some creative ideas we can use so we can move our organizations to act as consumers looking to engage with our brand?

Sell relationships: This is an area in which volunteer personalities will shine. Highlight successful relationships, between volunteers and clients, and volunteers and other staff. Sell the relationship attributes volunteers possess, from supporting staff and clients to volunteers' humor, good nature and sweet spirit.

Start a buzz: Play with viral ideas such as a volunteer challenge, volunteer game or other fun ways to engage. Do you want to showcase a volunteer who is a floater and has multiple roles? Set up a "Where's Volunteer Walter" game and post pictures of Walter at work. Explain the mission impact of each task he completes.

Marketing with a fun vibe grabs attention, but delivers a serious message. Highlighting volunteer impact through both serious and lighthearted updates captures attention in different ways but delivers the same message: Volunteers add value.

Offer trials: Are staff reluctant to accept volunteer help? Offer volunteers on a trial or rotating basis and remove the fear that if volunteers don't work out, staff will feel awful for rejecting them. Name the initiative something catchy, such as "Money Back Guaranteed," or "If you don't like your volunteer, you can return her after 30 days."

Offer incentives: Incentivize your vision of volunteer help by offering perks for any staff willing to give your volunteers a try. Ask your existing volunteers to gather coupons or gift certificates from businesses they frequent as the incentives. If your organization has a thrift or resale store, partner with the shop and offer a shopping spree.

Enlist believers: Staff who work well with volunteers are often the best spokespeople for your programs. Ask these staff members to speak on your program's behalf at a staff meeting and call it a three minute "satisfied customer" spot. The satisfied customer spot supports your role as an entrepreneur in charge of volunteer assets as we explored in step 3.

Make it cool or sexy: Can volunteerism be sexy? It can if you make the staff members who successfully work with volunteers cool and sexy. Craft messages which make those staff members look like they are cutting edge, ahead of everyone else and watch other staff want to mimic them.

Form a staff recruitment initiative: Equip them with "you are the volunteer we are looking for" business cards to hand out. Your staff knows firsthand the qualities you are seeking in a prospective volunteer, especially since you have sought staff's opinions and listened to their needs. Because you have included staff in crafting a "wish list" for volunteer talent in step 1, they will help you find good prospects. Award prizes for the most volunteers recruited.

Step 4 is reframing priorities and volunteer tasks must be prioritized under the definition, "Mission Centric Volunteer Engagement and Impact." How does each volunteer task further the mission? It is imperative you get administration on board with the concept, so approach senior management and ask them to partner with you in designing a **priority tasks principle**.

Include recommendations from key volunteers who know the challenges and rewards of volunteering firsthand. A **priority tasks principle** lists tasks in order of importance to the mission. Your priority task principle will look something like this:
- Direct client contact.
- Support work affecting clients.
- Tasks critical to daily operations.
- Fund raising tasks.
- Event tasks.
- Support work.
- Pilot programs.

When establishing organizational priorities, create a weighted system for volunteer requests. Assign a weight to tasks.

Most likely, anything client related will weigh high or first. Other highly weighted tasks will include the volunteer positions supporting the day to day running of the organization, e.g., the reception desk, phone monitoring, meal prep or other tasks necessary to keep a smooth and functioning operation.

Weight events according to size, stakeholder attendance, community participation or financial investment. In this model, a small health fair at a local worship center holds little weight against a yearly benefit attended by top donors.

Cross-reference priority weight by other factors such as timeliness of request, difficulties for the volunteers and the number of volunteers requested. Each of these ancillary conditions requires more volunteer manager time and must be weighted accordingly. For example, a request asking for 10 volunteers at a last-minute event takes a back seat to a request for 5 volunteers to help a client celebrate a birthday.

Develop a **mission centric volunteer request form** to assess the weight each request will carry. Use the form to gather information that reveals the weight of the request, such as:
- Date requested, date needed.
- Number of volunteers needed: What are the duties for each specific role?
- How does this further our mission?
- Which key stakeholders will be present?
- Does this job temporarily replace staff?
- Would we pay staff to do this job?
- The name of the staff member overseeing the volunteers.

Step 4 is creating a weighted task system that involves constraints. In **volunteer project management**, just as in project management, there are constraints on each component. Constraint variables affect expectations and results. The constraints placed on volunteer projects comprise:
- Volunteer resources (number of available volunteers at the time).
- Timeframe (how much time is allotted for the request to be filled).
- Skill levels (the volunteer skills requested).
- Scope (task instructions or goals).

The four constraints, when delivered as requested, results in a balanced project and meets expected results. However, when one or more of these constraints are out of balance, then original expectations must change.

Let's look at the four constraints that affect expectations in a volunteer project. They consist of:

Volunteer project resources: The available volunteers at the time. How many volunteers are actually available for the task? Refer back to step 2 for volunteer availability charts.

Volunteer project timeframe: The date of expected completion and by default, the amount of time allotted to complete all aspects.

Volunteer project skill level: The required volunteer skill sets or talents or any specific volunteer duties.

Volunteer project scope: The fleshed out or clear instructions or goals.

Each of these constraints impacts a volunteer project and can make or break the outcome. And, once one constraint is imbalanced, it directly affects the others.

For example, let's suppose the events team requests 5 volunteers for an important gala next month. They require the volunteers to have completed speaker bureau training as they will be serving as concierges for top donors. They request each volunteer to wear a white shirt and black slacks and show up on the evening of the event at 7pm.

Let's breakdown the request:
- 5 volunteers = volunteer project resources.
- Next month = volunteer project timeframe.
- Speakers' Bureau training required = volunteer project skill level.
- Wear a white shirt and black slacks, act as a concierge and be present at 7pm = volunteer project scope (instructions) which can sometimes be confusing or incomplete.

On initial examination, the four constraints seem reasonable. Engaging 5 volunteers with a month's notice who have had training and can start at 7pm wearing black slacks and white shirts is straightforward. But what if the constraints change as often happens to volunteer managers?

One week before the event, the volunteer manager is told that the events team needs 10 volunteers, and they must be at the event at 5pm. Constraints are now imbalanced. Resources (number of skilled volunteers) has changed. Timeframe (one week to implement changes) has also changed. Scope (be there at 5pm instead of 7pm) has also changed.

The volunteer manager cannot automatically produce 5 extra skilled volunteers in a week nor can all the scheduled volunteers arrive at 5pm instead of 7pm. The events team has to adjust their expectations.

Will some unskilled volunteers be acceptable in order to send 10 volunteers? Will sending 7 skilled volunteers be acceptable? Will it be acceptable for some volunteers to arrive at 7pm instead of 5pm?

Speak about **balanced volunteer projects,** especially when you are faced with volunteer requests that morph frequently or are not clear to begin with. Constantly having to rework a change is counterproductive. Imbalance does not allow a volunteer manager the time needed to sort out the changes.

Outline reasonable expectations and do not be afraid to state the compromises necessary to complete a project. This means keeping careful notes and records surrounding any blips. If a staff member calls and leaves a message changing a constraint, record the time and day in your project folder. Do not accept casual stops in the hallway by staff who throw monkey wrenches into your work.

Prioritize volunteer project management. Inform staff that a change to requests throws it into an imbalance and will cause altered expectations. By slotting volunteer involvement into **volunteer project management,** we give it an identity.

We must stop the merry-go-round system most organizations operate under in which imbalances fall onto the volunteer manager's shoulders while expectations remain the same.

Under the volunteer project management model, when changes occur, reset the timeframe from the original date to the date the changes are made. Then lower the priority level.

Staff cannot expect a volunteer manager to produce volunteers as if they are tools in a drawer. Let's revisit the above request for 5 volunteers with speaker's bureau training to act as concierges for a major event.

Once the event team requested changes, (10 volunteers instead of 5 who need to be at the event 2 hours earlier) the timeframe changes from one month to one week. It doesn't matter that one month was a very generous timeframe to begin with; it matters that the entire project was reset with a one week timeframe.

Why? Because the event team cannot expect the 5 volunteers originally recruited to all adapt to the new requirements nor can they expect the volunteer manager to produce 5 new volunteers. Essentially, the project is starting anew.

Based on your weighted system, you can internally publicize your priority task weights. Think of how much we track in our daily lives. You can track a pizza being made and delivered. You can track almost any package you ordered online.

Companies institute trackers to cut down on customers calling and asking when their order will arrive. Volunteer managers can take advantage of a tracking system to cut down on staff stopping in the hallway asking where you are on getting a volunteer for tomorrow. It also visually illustrates how constant changes to a volunteer project request reduces its priority status as you add the changes to the tracker and reset the timeframe.

Another advantage of creating a simple tracking system is it shows the occupied volunteers. If Jeb in accounting asks for two volunteers to input a large amount of data by Friday, he has no idea Rose asked for three volunteers to staff a Friday event while Marquis asked for a volunteer to walk a client's dog, also on Friday. There is no visual evidence your pool of volunteers dwindles every time a volunteer agrees to a task or has an ongoing assignment.

Post a chart of "requests in progress" in a shared drive or area where staff can track the progress on a **volunteer request tracker** (This is a great job for a key volunteer). Visually showing that last-minute or complicated requests hold lower priority than timely and well-designed requests will reinforce the need for requestors to be cognizant of timeframes, volunteer availability and the challenges in meeting complicated requests.

As a companion to your volunteer request tracker, add the **volunteer availability chart**. Remember, numbers are misleading. Saying there are 200 volunteers on the books means staff assumes you have 200 volunteers at your disposal every time they have a need. It's no wonder they don't understand why you cannot find a volunteer for a last-minute assignment.

We touched on this in step 2; the **volunteer track**. Again, group volunteers into categories such as "Client Volunteers," (add the required training they have received or are in the midst of receiving), "Event Volunteers," "Student Volunteers," "Emeritus Volunteers," "Volunteers in Development," and other categories breaking the numbers down into pools of availability from which you draw.

Add in the number of volunteers in each group already occupied with other requests. This is an eye-opener for staff who only think in terms of the number of overall volunteers. It is also a visual showing the many areas volunteers impact.

Step 4 is prioritizing Volunteer Role Scalability: This is the time to rework roles based on scalability. In business, scalability refers to a business's ability to increase or decrease production, depending upon need. But what is volunteer role scalability exactly? In simple terms, can you handle 5 volunteers or 20 volunteers at a time?

Let's first look at business scalability and this example: A toy maker introduces a new toy, Blammo and spends a lot of money on advertising Blammo, hoping to generate a buzz. The company floods the market with ads, touting Blammo as the toy all kids want.

However, the toy manufacturer quickly learns a lesson when advertising pays off, orders pour in for Christmas and they haven't accounted for scale. Woefully understaffed, they struggle to buy the materials needed and the equipment necessary to fill the orders. Production grinds to a halt. They fail to fill the orders before Christmas and face angry customers and a ruined reputation because they didn't plan their operation's scalability.

Does this sound eerily familiar to you? The increase in episodic, and corporate volunteer groups looking to engage in corporate social responsibility might be a volunteer manager's worst nightmare.

What do you do with 20 untrained, corporate volunteers who want to work five hours on a Saturday? Do you have scalable volunteer roles? Are you prepared to give them what they need while accomplishing something tangible for your organization or do you have to run around finding meaningless work for them to do?

Corporate volunteering is rapidly evolving into something more than just team building. It is increasingly about public image and meeting their employees' company vision, especially for millennials. Why would any company want to do that? Because employee satisfaction means an all-around improved workforce and improved public image means more sales. It is also about partnerships between businesses and the communities they profit from.

We may feel that corporate volunteering is not real, free-will volunteering and we can argue that point all day. However, the CSR trend is exponentially growing and we must prepare to work with it and stay ahead of it. It is an opportunity for leaders of volunteer engagement and impact to shine if we mold it to meet our needs.

Creating scalable volunteer roles is difficult. But, since corporate and episodic volunteering is on the rise, prioritizing the management of corporate and episodic involvement will make your volunteer engagement and impact program better in the long run and keep you from the headache of not knowing what to do when a group contacts you.

Start small and then, as you take control and record successes, forge partnerships with companies. Partnerships will benefit the corporate partner (they have a proven location in which to engage in meaningful CSR) and your mission (engaged corporate partners will expand their connection to mission goals).

Look for scalable roles. What can a group of people do? Poll staff for a wish list of projects. Does the building need pressure washing or painting? Do the grounds need weeding? These are common roles for groups to start a corporate experience.

But asking may produce other, more engaging wish list activities. Ask key staff, "If you have a group of say, 5 people, what could they help you with?"

If your organization includes a thrift store, the opportunities there abound. Can a group of people put up a seasonal display? Can they build boutique style dressing rooms? Save some of these wish list items for your corporate volunteers.

Require the benefiting department to be present to help manage the group and to speak about the impact on the mission. Emphasize no one knows how to complete the job nor what the impact will be more than the person(s) requesting the help.

Fashion roles for episodic volunteers to do outside your organization. What about creating their own fundraiser? Can they put together a group to enter a walk/run on your behalf? How about asking students to write valentine cards to clients? Can a corporate group adopt a family for a holiday?

Once you have a list of episodic roles, then determine scale. What is the ideal number of volunteers for each group activity? How many are too many or too few? You now have your **group range** for episodic volunteering opportunities.

Write up a menu of volunteer activities to give interested groups. Outline the constraints upfront, such as "the activity is available during the week from M-F," or "this activity is available on Saturday mornings."

Make any requirements clear, for example, "volunteer groups must bring their own shovels and garden gloves." Add in a FAQ (frequently asked questions) section with answers. For example:

- "Are refreshments provided? A: We will provide water for 10 volunteers."
- "Does the volunteer site have restrooms? A: There is access to bathroom facilities on the first floor."

Use your marketing skills and add enticing highlights to each menu item. Speak in specifics to mission impact and benefits to illustrate why this group activity is important.

Phrases such as "this is team building," or "your valuable time will be well spent," are broad, almost meaningless phrases. If one of your item menu offerings is weeding the garden in front of your shelter, add in a blurb stating why this is important.

For example, "The serenity garden in front of the shelter is the first thing our clients see when they arrive. A beautiful garden is a visual welcome and makes them feel a little less unsure. We explain the meaning of each flower to help ease their fears."

Above all, find true impact in each corporate volunteering activity and prepare to show that impact in concrete terms. Just like individual volunteers, corporate groups will only waste their efforts on meaningless jobs one time. It is better to turn away groups at the outset then to go through starts and stops with companies because a corporate outing failed due to lack of preparation, meaningful activity or a poorly executed plan.

So, how important is prioritizing episodic volunteer groups by creating activities beforehand, scaling roles and creating menus? Which of these two group experiences do you think shows strategic planning and has potential for a continuing partnership?

A corporate group approaches volunteer manager Elliot with a request to do an activity for 10 volunteers on Saturday. Elliot agrees because he's afraid that if he turns them down, they will complain to his CEO. He scrambles to find an activity for the group by calling every department in his organization.

Finally, he speaks to the head of maintenance who says the group can weed the front garden. Elliot calls the corporate group leader and leaves a message on voicemail. "We're all set. Come in on Saturday."

The group arrives on Saturday, but with 20 people, as 10 more employees joined at the last minute. Taken by surprise, Elliot tells the group leader he could only scrape together enough gloves and tools for 10 people so he runs back to his office to find something for the other 10 people to do.

He returns with a current list of his volunteers and asks the group to divide into two groups of 10 people each. He takes the first group into the garden while the second group sits and waits for him to return. They look at their watches and chat until Elliot comes back inside.

He shepherds them into a conference room where he gives them the volunteer list along with a stack of note cards and asks them to write thank you cards to the volunteers. He writes a generic message for them to copy on the whiteboard at the front of the room.

After 10 minutes, the group has finished the cards and passes the time by checking email. A flustered Elliot returns and informs the group it is their turn to weed. They go outside, but now the other 10 people have nothing to do inside.

After a few more minutes, while Elliot is running around trying to find something else, the weeding is done and all 20 people are idly standing in the lobby, so Elliot ushers them into a meeting room and plays his volunteer recruitment video. He breaks open the water and asks them to share, apologizing for not having enough. When the video is over, the group leaves.

Meanwhile, a corporate group of 10 approaches volunteer manager Flavia, looking to volunteer on a Saturday. Flavia emails a menu of available activities to the group leader. She highlights the two activities scalable for 10 people on a Saturday. The group chooses an activity and Flavia sets up a time to meet the group two Saturdays later.

The group, having brought their own tools as stipulated on the menu, arrives and gets to work. Flavia has provided snacks and water as per the FAQ section of the menu.

After the group finishes the weeding, Flavia ushers the group into a room where two volunteers and a client's family member await. They present impact stories on how volunteering has helped the organization's clients with anecdotal references to "getting a sense of peace from seeing the beautiful garden you just weeded."

Flavia invites the group to take volunteer orientation and offers to conduct training on company premises. A week later, Flavia's CEO sends a thank-you letter to the group's leader and invites them back for another group activity at their convenience. Her CEO adds the corporation to the organizational mailing list.

Step 4 is prioritizing the creation of a corporate and episodic volunteering strategy. We must be proactive and prioritize being prepared versus rushing about to find things to do when a group contacts us. Spend priority time designing your corporate volunteering strategy by seeking wish list items and off-site opportunities. Take control and search for a corporate partner with shared values and don't wait for a business to contact you. By forging relationships on your terms you will build a stronger partnership.

Do not be afraid to say to businesses, clubs or teams, "no, this doesn't fit in with what we offer, but let me show you what we have." Explain that by manufacturing a last-minute activity, the participants will have a poor experience and as a leader of volunteer engagement and impact, your aim is to involve all volunteers, even those who volunteer episodically in meaningful, impactful work.

Constructing a menu of group activities shows forethought. So many groups show up at organizations, ready to volunteer and find that not only is there little for them to do, but they've just heaped pressure on a harried volunteer manager. It's a bad experience for everyone.

Corporate employees, club and team members are familiar with rules and regulations. Expect them to adhere to yours. Take only the groups who fit with the activities you have available. Remember, spinning your wheels and wasting precious time trying to manufacture a group activity you can't scale properly is not a priority. It doesn't further your vision. It isn't mission centric. It won't establish partnerships with corporations. In the big picture, it won't instill volunteering in anyone.

If someone from your senior management team or another staff member approaches you and asks you to make up an activity for their son's soccer team, hand her/him the menu. Be prepared to stick to your plan and explain how you have put together the best experience for everyone involved. Explain that meaningful volunteer tasks forge partnerships that last. Refer to group volunteering as **engaged and impactful group volunteering.**

Most groups sincerely want to help and most teachers and coaches want their students and players to learn a valuable life lesson. Volunteer managers understand this element, so in developing youth group activities, take the learning experience into consideration. What will the group learn or experience? Add the tangible takeaways on your menu, such as learning about your organization's work, discovering a new skill or exploring leadership possibilities.

When a group has completed their volunteer project or day of volunteering, enlist your CEO to write a thank-you letter. Offer to write the letter for her/his signature. Remember our priority is developing **key volunteers.**

With clubs, teams and corporate volunteer partners, we are developing **key partnerships.** Just as our volunteer investors bring so much more than the hours we record, group partners will invest more than a volunteering day.

As the **leader of the volunteer engagement and impact program,** prioritize capturing the "other" ways in which key partners invest in your organization by tracking donations, newsletter blurbs and employee awareness of your mission.

Send an evaluation form after the group has completed their volunteering activity to analyze which aspects of the project work and which do not. You can even include a question on the form asking, "Would you be open to exploring volunteering further?" List new opportunities and offer to conduct volunteer training at their site. Follow up with the group's leader after a time and ask for constructive feedback.

In step 3, we explored **key volunteers** and **volunteer accounts**. While designing priorities, spend more of your time with your key volunteers. These are the volunteers who you have designated as those contributing a huge share of the important work being done; the 80/20 rule in which 80% of impact comes from 20% of your volunteer capital. Ask staff to help you identify key volunteers. Including staff in elevating volunteers to key status gives staff more "buy-in" when you speak of spending priority time with these select volunteers and encourages staff to invest in keeping them coming back.

Step 4 is prioritizing time management. Develop key volunteers as **volunteer leaders.** Each key volunteer who can take on volunteer initiatives, mentor new volunteers, help you (with stats, surveys, follow-ups, etc.) or recruit new volunteers exponentially increases your ability to handle the workload and frees you to take on projects that align with your vision. Don't make becoming indispensable your goal. Instead, focus on efforts moving your program forward while delegating responsibilities to key volunteers.

Delegate more and prioritize your volunteer department over putting others ahead of your own needs. Most volunteer managers get excited when a new volunteer with exceptional skills comes onboard because they immediately think of how much this volunteer can aid finance or marketing or administration.

But what about keeping some of these cream of the crop volunteers for yourself? Don't skimp on your needs. Assemble a team of highly engaged and talented volunteers to help you accomplish your goals.

Spend your time wisely with sporadic volunteers. The idea that volunteer managers must stop everything to engage all people who call, stop in, or inquire about volunteering just keeps the volunteer manager working in a daily state of chaos.

Prioritizing means managing time for the most benefit. Chasing down prospective volunteers is counterproductive.

Before you counter with "but each volunteer is unique and you never know who will be a great volunteer," please let me explain. I too, have experienced great volunteers coming from hesitant starts. I don't mean engaging prospective volunteers who show potential is counterproductive, I mean chasing prospective volunteers who show limited interest is counterproductive.

Spending vast amounts of time talking to people into volunteering doesn't set a firm foundation. The prospective volunteer must undertake responsibility for volunteering or else they have no buy-in and even if you get them to sign on, you will lose them quickly.

You may find someone wants to volunteer but they are hesitant or insecure or unsure of what to expect. For those volunteers, you encourage them and help them understand that they can do it. I've found that some of my most effective volunteers were unsure in the beginning. But they at least wanted to try.

Your priority in managing time must be to engage the serious volunteer. If you still feel as though every person who inquires needs attention, then assign a caring key volunteer to work with prospective volunteers. This way, you can spend your time moving forward.

Check emails once or twice a day at most. Ask a key volunteer to answer your phone and take messages. Use calendars and block time for working on goal-oriented initiatives. Prioritize getting volunteer help to manage your tasks.

Step 4 is professionalizing your time. Wean staff and volunteers from an open-door policy to more manageable scheduled interactions. Publicize your calendar and block out the times you are developing and engaging volunteers. If we don't appear to treat volunteer engagement and impact as a profession needing uninterrupted blocks of time, then no one else will either.

Use professional terms to explain volunteer engagement activities so staff and volunteers don't assume you are just socializing and think nothing of interrupting you.

Instead of leaving the door open while describing the time spent with volunteer Sarah as a "chat," post a sign on your door illustrating the HR (human resources) function of your job. Use terms relating to retention, mentoring, recruiting from within (**internal recruitment**) and mediating when speaking about time spent with volunteers. Use terms such as:

Policy review in session: Volunteers often question procedures or need guidance on an acceptable course of action. Thank goodness they check in with us before going "Lone Ranger" and doing whatever they feel is best. The more time we spend explaining policies, the less time we spend fixing mistakes. Educate staff on the importance of these one-on-one volunteer meetings, whether scheduled or impromptu.

Volunteer annual review and goal setting: Reviews are normal HR functions. Volunteers are no different and need individualized time with us so they can receive valuable feedback and set goals for future volunteering.

Volunteer stay interview: We may sense a volunteer losing interest or having a difficult time or we want to make sure our volunteers aren't thinking of leaving. A stay interview is volunteer retention at its best. Every interaction we have with a volunteer is an attempt to get them to stay, including listening to their family stories, hearing their jokes or looking at pictures from their trips. Volunteer stay interviews occur every day.

Volunteer collaboration: Sometimes we need to step in and spend time with a volunteer before an issue gets out of hand.

Volunteer planning: You may wish to sit down with a staff member and plan out volunteer involvement.

Volunteer mediation: When a conflict arises between a volunteer and another volunteer or a staff member, we must mediate so all sides can work towards a satisfactory solution. It takes multiple interactions to ensure each party can move on and support organizational goals.

Volunteer internal, targeted recruitment: It takes deft persuasion to fill certain tasks. Targeted recruitment is the time spent recruiting an existing volunteer or a new volunteer for specific or difficult tasks. Emphasize the skills needed to introduce existing volunteers to new volunteering avenues. Organizations assume that once a volunteer comes onboard, they will do anything asked of them. Internal recruitment means refreshing a volunteer's original enthusiasm and guiding them to go deeper in their support.

Volunteer assignment or task review: Volunteers need periodic checking in to determine their satisfaction level or if they are having issues with their assigned task.

The point is, if we wish that others knew all the different functions we use to engage volunteers, then we must identify the work. Think about the difference between these two conversations:

CEO: "Karen, I tried to call you but you didn't answer."

Karen: "I'm sorry. I had a volunteer in my office."

CEO: "They were in with you for 30 minutes."

Karen: "I know, I, uh, we were talking."

CEO: "I need you to work on volunteer requests, not socialize."

Now let's compare that conversation to this one:

CEO: "Jamal, I tried to call you but you didn't answer."

Jamal: "I'm sorry. I was engaged in a volunteer task review."

CEO: "Volunteer task review, what is that?"

Jamal: "It is reviewing task expectations with a volunteer. We go over any updates or changes, feedback from staff and also the volunteer's satisfaction and input."

CEO: "Oh, I didn't realize you did that. How's that going?"

Jamal: "Really well. The review serves to make sure the volunteer is meeting staff expectations and it intercepts problems before they become challenging. It also gives the volunteers a chance to voice any concerns and reinforces the team aspect."

CEO: "I'm impressed."

Perceptions, especially deeply ingrained perceptions reinforce when we continue to operate in the mode that created those perceptions. Volunteer management priorities must include revising how we explain and present engaging volunteers so that perceptions shift towards viewing engaging volunteers as a profession with specific duties and skills.

Step 4 is streamlining processes. Streamlining processes and maximizing results will yield more time for engaging key volunteers, recruiting new key volunteers, creating initiatives and developing a professional department vital to the mission.

What processes and/or work can you streamline so priorities take precedence? This is an area in which volunteers are most helpful. Form a **volunteer task force** made up of your key volunteers to review volunteer applications, volunteer reporting forms, volunteer interviews, placement procedures, meetings, mentoring, training, disciplinary proceedings and questions.

Give the task force free rein to review processes and make recommendations. Volunteer task forces are think tanks comprising experienced and new volunteers who, together will share their perspectives and make recommendations on improving your systems.

It is not our goal to make volunteering easier, but rather our goal is to streamline the process so every prospective volunteer can onboard in a timely and unencumbered manner. Other streamlined processes will ensure that existing volunteers don't waste precious time in overly burdensome reviews or meetings.

Step 4 is reframing reports to reflect priorities. Measuring success in the non-profit world has always been difficult, especially in the volunteer sector. How can you accurately measure a calming presence or empathy? The intimate relationships that volunteers form with clients is profound and somehow, it feels wrong to squeeze these impactful moments into cold statistics.

And so, because helping metrics were difficult to identify, volunteer coordinators kept using the old methods of recording hours spent and money saved to explain volunteer impact.

In business, the KPI, or **key performance indicator** measures the results of activities crucial to an organization or business. As you work towards **mission centric volunteer engagement and impact** and assess the volunteer department priorities, the question then becomes, "how can we measure the results of our concentration on mission centric volunteer engagement and impact?" Crafting a **key performance indicator for volunteer engagement and impact (KPI-VEI)** is the answer.

Go back to your priority task principle. The key performance indicator mirrors the levels of mission centric volunteer contributions versus lumping all volunteer hours together. Using a key performance indicator aids you in showing how volunteers impacted mission goals.

It sheds light on where your volunteer manager focus needs to be centered. The difference between reporting on volunteer hours versus reporting on key performance indicators is this: While all volunteer work helps the organization, key performances further the mission.

The first step in crafting the KPI-VEI is to gain access to any client surveys your organization sends out during or after a client and family uses your services. What questions appear on the survey?

For some organizations, there may be a general question on volunteer satisfaction which you can track. But there's a more important statistic to track: Overall satisfaction of a family who availed themselves of volunteer help versus those who did not.

I heard about a very astute volunteer manager who tracked those statistics and her curiosity paid off. The surveys from the clients who partook of volunteer help *significantly showed a higher level of satisfaction across the board* than the clients who received no volunteer help. While this comes as no surprise to volunteer managers, it is an eye-opening statistic that supports our contention that volunteers add real value.

For organizations who send out satisfaction surveys, this cause (volunteer help) and effect (higher satisfaction across the board) is critical to understanding volunteer impact. Volunteers add a significant layer of satisfaction due to the time they spend with clients by listening, reinforcing and attending to needs.

Your KPI-VEI, when based on organizational survey data will feature clients' well-being and satisfaction related to the number of volunteers involved, hours spent and roles filled. Pick out the questions you can relate to volunteer impact such as "did you feel as though our organization met your needs" and reflect that on your impact report: 12 clients reported having their needs met by 12 volunteers who contributed 87 hours by driving clients to doctors' appointments.

Another way to enact a KPI-VEI report is to break client satisfaction down into the specific benefits a client received by volunteer participation. In place of recording only the hours spent with a client, record the specific impact each hour had on supporting the client.

For direct client contact, how many clients retained their independence, or did not have to hire someone, or had satisfactory outcomes because of volunteers? You will find clinical staff's client evaluations a wealth of information you can use in impact reports.

For key events, how many donors or stakeholders were impacted because volunteers were greeters, or helped set up? How much money was raised at an event staffed by volunteers?

For volunteers who fill in for staff, how much money was saved because volunteers, *who were already familiar with organizational culture and could fill in seamlessly*, took on these roles instead of the organization having to hire temporary help who had limited experiences interacting with vulnerable populations?

How many staff hours did volunteers save, thus giving staff time to do other, important work? And what other mission centric work were they able to accomplish?

The reporting statistics look like this:

- Because three volunteers spent 40 hours last month on mandated paperwork, our five clinical staff spent 40 more hours in direct client support.
- Because a volunteer spent 20 hours last month making follow-up phone calls, clinical staff was able to spend 20 more hours during client visits.

A **volunteer impact report** that captures the above data illustrates volunteer value and contributions. Move towards results, changes and progress versus relying on hours to tell the volunteer impact story. As for gathering statistics showcasing the intangibles, such as empathy or calming presence, use your phone surveys, the ones mentioned in step 2.

Ask specific and measurable questions of clients and families, for example, "How has our volunteer, Jean helped you personally?" Pull out the impact verbs such as "listens to me," "supports me," or "cares about me," or "allowed me to keep going to yoga class," and turn them into statistical data.

How do we turn these phrases into data?

- Listens to me becomes clients felt their concerns were heard.
- Supports me becomes clients felt supported.
- Cares for me becomes clients' wellbeing increased.
- Allowed me to keep going to yoga becomes client's quality of life increased or was supported.

Break reports and stats into smaller increments so end-of-year reports are easier to assemble when you need them. **Micro-level metrics** is a way to measure smaller goals. Combine them at the end of the year in an end-of-year report.

Break volunteering into micro levels. Not only are these stats easily digested, they give you continuous "wins" you can include in your **building the future of volunteer engagement and impact updates** from step 1. Micro-level metrics are the continuous statistics proving the success of your **volunteer engagement and impact program**. Share them often.

Metrics such as the number of volunteers who offered to help launch a program is a measurable number. Number of people who applied to be a volunteer this month is a measurable metric. Number of volunteers who completed an important training is measurable. Number of requests filled for the week is also measurable. Breaking metrics into smaller increments (weekly or even daily) makes recording larger metrics (monthly and yearly) less stressful and more accurate.

Cast metrics against expectations in a **Goal setting report**. What do you hope to accomplish next year? An increase in volunteers by 10%? Clients served by 5%? Volunteer retention by 10% over the previous year?

Measure results against expectations and apply the influencing factors to the results. If the increase in volunteers was +11%, the influencing factors might include a streamlined application process or the addition of new volunteer roles, or a newsletter. (Surveys or reviews can capture measurable influencers as can initial volunteer interviews). But what if say, volunteers retained decreased by 4%, do you sweep this statistic under the rug and not report it?

No, instead, look for the reasons it decreased. What if organizational policies changed and volunteers were no longer allowed to fill certain roles they had previously filled? What if volunteers did not find a meaningful fit? Statistics reflecting causation are always worth reporting because they support your claims and support your push for more resources or adjustments.

Stats are eye-opening, and point to **cause** (organizational changes or lack of meaningful roles) and **effect** (volunteers quit). Use cause-and-effect statistics to back up your observances such as volunteers want flexible schedules (keep track of why volunteers leave with exit interviews or surveys), or volunteers do not want a volunteer appreciation luncheon but want meaningful recognition (graph the declining participation at the luncheon and gather volunteer opinions).

Step 4 is reframing priorities which means a more targeted approach to volunteer recruitment. How do we target the people we believe will further our mission and become key volunteers? Is there a volunteer prototype? A helpful exercise is one in which you construct your ideal volunteer by jotting down characteristics and availability. Add in where this ideal volunteer lives and how much time they will devote to volunteering.

Conceptualize the ideal volunteer by sketching or naming him/her. Let's call him Damon. Who is Damon? Construct an ideal volunteer for each task you need to fill and then plan a **targeted recruitment strategy**.

How do you appeal to your ideal volunteer Damon? What is he like? What does his day look like? What about his connection to your organization? Or his needs? What would attract a volunteer like Damon?

Talk about targeted recruitment when discussing volunteer roles with staff and senior management. Enlist them in creating "Damons" for the roles volunteers fill in their departments. Put up "Damon wanted" flyers throughout your organization and encourage your staff to be on the lookout for potential "Damons."

Find an existing key volunteer who matches many of your targeted volunteer traits and enlist their help. Find out what motivates them and what brought them to you in the first place. Ask them to help you write ads they would take the time to answer.

Step 4 is determining vision. What is a vision? A vision not only determines the things most important to you, it also shapes your values and direction. It gives you the opportunity to strategize how you will form your ideal initiative. Take a moment now and stop whatever you are doing because this is important. Clear your mind and think about your vision for your **volunteer engagement and impact program**. Where do you see it going? What do you envision your program looks like in a perfect world?

Framing a vision is not about using the first ideas that pop into your head. It takes careful thought and as you construct a vision in your mind, you will see the direction you wish to take your program. Write your ideas down and go back and revise them until you have a **volunteer program vision statement.**

A departmental vision statement must be on the top of your priority list. You may find you pen a simple statement like "volunteers are respected and treated well." While broad, this vision serves to illustrate the most important goal you have for your initiative.

Or you might have a longer statement that includes "increasing volunteer satisfaction, involving volunteers in strategic positions, recruiting key volunteers, embracing diversity and inclusion, developing leadership roles and improving methods of reporting statistics."

Take the time to ponder your idea of a thriving **volunteer engagement and impact program**. Let the ideas flow. Think of all the vision pieces working together, then pick out each component and examine it. These components may include:

- Volunteers recognized for their contributions.
- Freedom to take on projects showcasing volunteer abilities.
- The leader of volunteer role included in senior management and strategic planning.
- Volunteers in leadership roles.
- Resources to further innovative ideas.

While in their purest form, the components of a perfect volunteer world might seem unreachable or too broad, but as you write them down, they become tangible. How can these components break down into smaller, more manageable goals? How can your vision come to life, one step at a time? Where do these goals intersect?

Creating a **strategic volunteer initiative vision plan** is not just busy work. Once you have your concrete vision in hand, then you can mold everything you say and do in terms of how it furthers your vision.

For example, if your vision includes recognition of volunteer impact, then keep that vision component in the forefront of your mind, so you begin to politely and professionally guide staff into meaningful volunteer value recognition.

Let's look at how this works. A staff member says to you in passing, "Our volunteer Janice helped a lot when she came in last minute to get our invitation out to donors."

Instead of saying, "thanks, I'll pass that along," go back to your meaningful volunteer recognition vision and ask the staff member, "how does the invitation Janice mailed out impact our mission?"

Add in, "We need to let Janice know her hard work furthered our goals, so if you can give me some stats on how much money this helped raise, I will pass them on to her." And, as a bonus, use these statistics later for impact reports.

By hearkening back to your vision of **volunteer value recognition**, you will not only be implementing it, you will plant a new normal in the minds of staff. They will think of volunteer recognition in the way you have outlined it.

Replacing habits with new habits takes repeating, so weave your vision into everything you say and do. This is leadership at its best. It takes determination to reshape culture, but consistency is key to changing habits to match your vision.

One of your vision components may be to start a new and innovative volunteer role. You may have volunteers who are not interested in traditional roles or you may seek to involve people who rarely answer your ads. Here, innovation will achieve your vision.

Let's say you want to harness the passion you see in social justice warriors. They are non-traditional compared to other volunteers in your program, but they can be instrumental in helping your volunteer team increase in diversity and inclusion. Instead of thinking about recruiting these warriors for traditional roles, appeal to their zeal for justice and ask them to help you devise tangible ways your organization can move towards inclusion.

Step 4 is prioritizing your unique and important role. If your volunteer engagement and impact vision contains no personal goals, it is incomplete. Remember, impactful teams need a visionary guide. As the leader of volunteer engagement and impact, it is your critical role that defines the success of your program, so do not skimp on personal development. Make time to ensure that your growth, both professionally and personally is central to your vision. Consider yourself a crucial tool to your program's success, one that requires sharpening.

Visionary leaders take care to stretch their minds and abilities to keep moving. Along with professionalizing your initiative, seek inclusion in management trainings and educational opportunities offered by your organization. Advocate for your inclusion in leadership development.

By this step, your professionalism and progressive solutions should be clear and the improvements you are making should be leverage enough to ask for the personal development you seek. Have the courage and confidence to speak of the steps you have taken to improve volunteer engagement and impact and be confident in requesting leadership development.

It is now time to advocate for inclusion in planning volunteer roles and involvement. Remember keeping track of personal accomplishments in Step 3? Prepare a report highlighting all you have accomplished.

Devise an elevator speech which pinpoints the reasons you should be at planning sessions. Bring your examples of mission impact. Don't be afraid to ask for endorsements from departments who have benefited from your visionary leadership. Step up and offer your expert opinion on how to more efficiently accomplish a goal with volunteer help.

Especially point to any volunteer projects that moved the organization forward or helped reduce challenges. This is a key reason you should be at the planning table. Your leadership input is vital to your organization's success.

When you feel as though you have a solid vision in mind and have set your priorities, then it's time to lead a movement.

Step 4 Checklist:
- ✓ Reframe priorities
- ✓ Rebrand volunteers
- ✓ Elevate volunteer impact
- ✓ Recognize volunteer synergy
- ✓ Embrace potential
- ✓ Prioritize mission centric tasks
- ✓ Create weighted task system involving constraints
- ✓ Prioritize volunteer role scalability
- ✓ Prioritize group volunteering strategy
- ✓ Prioritize time management
- ✓ Professionalize your time
- ✓ Streamline processes
- ✓ Reframe reports to reflect priorities
- ✓ Develop targeted volunteer recruitment
- ✓ Determine your vision
- ✓ Prioritize your role

Step 5: Reframing Volunteer Retention as Sustainable Volunteering

Jazmine looked across the dinner table at her husband, Dwayne. He studied her for a moment and asked, "What's the matter tonight, you seem down?"

She picked at her plate. "It's volunteering. I don't know if I want to do it anymore."

Dwayne nodded. "I have noticed lately that you're not excited to go. Jaz, you're doing so much already. You've got work and school and you help me take care of my mom. Maybe you should give it up."

"But I love the place. I love what they do."

"I know." Dwayne set his fork down. "Then what it is?"

Jazmine took a breath. "I don't love what I do there anymore. I'm learning so much in my marketing course." Her eyes brightened, "and I know I can really make a difference putting a new marketing plan in place."

"Then ask them to move you to the marketing department."

"I did. They said marketing doesn't have an opening right now and I was too valuable and I know my current job better than anyone. That's the problem. I'm stuck."

"Then quit."

Jazmine sighed. "I might have to."

Recruitment and retention have always been the cornerstone of volunteer management. In simplest form, recruitment and retention is rather like an assembly line; we recruit volunteers, push them down the task conveyor belt and then we make them stay. So linear, right?

But over the past couple of decades, volunteer retention hasn't been so easy, especially because the volunteer management conveyor belt is getting rusty and as we've discovered, volunteering doesn't follow a linear path. Volunteers aren't staying like they used to.

We've been trying to grease the conveyor belt gears with appreciation events, awards and newsletters but it's not working. Is it because we're not trying hard enough or is something else at play? Well, let's ask this question: What is a definition of recruitment and retention, anyway?

Volunteer Recruitment is the act of finding volunteers to join. It is pretty straightforward.

Volunteer Retention is the continued control or possession of volunteers. Oh, that's a problem. Retention is an antiquated notion. Let's try a different word.

Volunteer Sustainability is the ability to maintain volunteers at a certain level or the avoidance of the depletion of volunteers to maintain an ecological balance for all.

In the current norm, organizations consider the retention of volunteers a function of the volunteer department, so volunteer managers hold themselves accountable for volunteers who leave. The volunteer's departure directly relates to a volunteer coordinator's efforts.

When a volunteer moves on, implied fingers can point at the volunteer coordinator and their actions, as if no other reason could possibly explain why a volunteer would quit. 'Doing good work,' even menial work is enough to keep volunteers not only coming back, but enough to inspire volunteers to do more, no matter what obstacles are in their way.

But once volunteers join, the volunteer coordinator understands how precarious it is to keep volunteers involved and engaged. Volunteers leave for a myriad of reasons. Circumstances change, they fall ill, or they move or care for a loved one. Their finances dip, or they get married or divorced or they can't drive anymore.

Occasionally, something happens to make the volunteer frustrated or angry and sometimes volunteers need to move on or tackle a different activity. Long-term volunteers might feel they have done enough and their work is complete. They may have convinced themselves they have done what they set out to do, and it is time to do something else.

No matter the reason(s), volunteers are currently treated as possessions and are kept for usage whenever the need for their services arise. Filling tasks is enough to keep them engaged.

Volunteer coordinators have bent themselves into pretzels trying to educate their organizations on their volunteer force's fluidity, but it hasn't yet resonated. The "we must keep all volunteers" mantra forced volunteer managers to do everything in their power to make volunteers "happy." Volunteer coordinators accepted volunteers who were not a good fit and spent precious time with people who had no intention of following through on promises.

For years, volunteer coordinators threw parties, asked staff to treat volunteers with respect and gratitude, smoothed over ruffled feathers and mediated when a volunteer wanted to quit because they were misunderstood. The notion that a volunteer coordinator's job was to hang on to every volunteer for all time became ingrained and systemic.

At the same time, how did organizations view their staff? Never was staff considered irreplaceable or kept at all costs. Staff retired, moved, found other jobs, changed circumstances, were fired or phased out. This disconnect between viewing staff as real people with free will and volunteers as tools perpetuated and grew over time.

Organizations have regarded the pool of available community citizens as deep and never ending. They never imagined a person who had time on their hands might not want to spend their free time volunteering.

It was easy for organizational leaders passionate about their work to assume the average citizen would display the same passion for mission goals and want to jump on the bandwagon and help. Why wouldn't they, if properly asked?

They regarded the volunteer coordinator who suggested not all people wanted to volunteer as a negative or lazy thinker. After all, a person with a few hours to spare would always say yes when a cheery volunteer coordinator asked them to volunteer, right? It really was that simple, wasn't it?

And yet, volunteer coordinators, through their accumulated extensive experience, realized that people who had a lot of time on their hands might have all that time on their hands because they wanted to keep it that way. Unfortunately, volunteer coordinators haven't made enough inroads when explaining the nuances governing volunteer recruitment and retention.

I can remember sharing national volunteering statistics with senior management. I presented a national report showing Florida consistently ranked near the bottom in percentage of population that volunteered.

"Impossible," a senior manager said. "We have more retired people here than anybody has."

I pointed to the research outlining the reasons Floridians were volunteering less than other states. Transplanted retirees had little connection to their new communities and volunteer organizations were not just competing with one other for retirees' time, we were competing with golf, tennis, the beach and a host of other leisure activities.

The room went silent and senior management stared at me. They took my explanation as an excuse for not getting hundreds more volunteers. That's where I went wrong and I hope you don't do what I did. Remember, in the pre-step, disrupting ourselves and the light bulb moment when my wise friend told me if I wanted others to change, I had to change?

Instead of only showing the back-up statistics on why it was difficult to recruit and retain retirees, I should have approached it differently. In hindsight, I should have first outlined all the positive statistics on volunteering (such as our increase in volunteer participation and new programs) and then said, "Despite this trend here in Florida, we are accomplishing some great things. Let me show you what they are."

The danger in explaining the reasons something is difficult is it sounds like you are making excuses and it doesn't offer solutions. When pointing out difficulties in volunteer management, temper the challenges with examples of solutions and results.

But back to the conveyor belt model. Organizations assumed recruitment should be ongoing, no matter how circumstances hindered success and never thought about the possibility that too many volunteers on paper was an impossible challenge to manage. Organizations equated more volunteers with automatically filling unpopular tasks. Conventional wisdom said a volunteer coordinator should keep recruiting until positions were filled.

No one saw the continuous internal recruitment that volunteer coordinators were engaged in to persuade existing volunteers into taking on more challenging or unappealing roles. Instead, organizations assumed that a volunteer coordinator recruited new volunteers for each task and it didn't take much work to match or develop a volunteer who engaged with vulnerable populations. There was little understanding nor appreciation for volunteer development.

The fluidity in number of volunteers plagued volunteer managers in unfair ways. Organizational hierarchy would hold the number of volunteers over a volunteer manager's head and complain, "If we have 100 volunteers, why can't we get one to file?"

So, volunteer coordinators found themselves in a no-win situation and lived in a non-profit Goldilocks and the Three Bears' world. Having too few volunteers meant they were not spending enough time recruiting and too many volunteers meant they weren't successful in convincing volunteers to take on tasks. How many volunteers were just right?

This continuous pressure to recruit weighed heavily on volunteer coordinators and unfortunately hatched a mindset to grab as many potential volunteers as possible. However, sheer numbers didn't produce volunteers who would take on tasks no one wanted. More volunteers on the books didn't mean they would commit to regular hours either. Instead of viewing volunteers as people with preferences, organizations kept expecting the "right volunteer" to come along.

Meanwhile, it was the volunteer coordinators who practiced matching volunteers to roles and realized that volunteers' interests, motivations and skills determined volunteer synergy. Higher numbers had no bearing on whether tasks were filled. And, instead of understanding the need to alter the task, organizations encouraged the volunteer manager to find the "right" volunteer.

The **volunteer talent churn** continued to haunt volunteer coordinators, and they struggled to scoop up every volunteer they could, hoping that one of the new volunteers would fill a task no one wanted to do. Sometimes they got "lucky" and a new volunteer agreed to try out a previously shunned task. Unfortunately these random, short-lived successes cemented the notion that constant recruiting for the right volunteer was what volunteer managers had to do. This occasional "luck" prevented organizations from redesigning volunteer engagement and instead, they shifted the reasons for empty volunteer roles onto lack of recruiting.

The flip side of excessive volunteer recruiting was many new volunteers had to wait for plum assignments to open because they wanted a role other than those offered. Volunteers who wanted to help a mission they believed in, signed up expecting to find a fit, but never got started.

And so, it became a numbers game. How many volunteers did you recruit this month? As if volunteers were berries picked in a field, numbers became the goal. How many hours did the volunteers contribute this month? Organizations equated hours with dollars saved as if organizations would have willingly spent money on staff if a volunteer wasn't there to do the job.

This numbers game destroyed any potential for creating a thriving network of volunteers and kept volunteer coordinators from time spent thoughtfully engaging potential **key volunteers**. Clinging to the status quo kept volunteer managers from developing impactful volunteer roles. Linear thinking wasted the enormous volunteer potential.

Focusing on hours gave us a numbers-aware volunteer coordinator. Many volunteers are lax in recording hours, mainly because they feel it's an unnecessary component of their work. Volunteer coordinators hounded volunteers to get hours recorded and were forced to equate number of volunteer hours with missions served. And, to add another layer of figures unrelated to impact, volunteer hours became equated with dollars saved in an attempt to validate volunteer work.

Unfortunately, these numbers became the ingrained way to assess volunteer contributions. Fully engaged key volunteers were lumped in with other names on a paper. Deeply impactful work was nothing more than two hours on a spreadsheet. Playing this numbers game shackled volunteer coordinators to meaningless statistics rather than unleashing them to further mission goals.

What was a dedicated volunteer coordinator to do? Become volunteer greedy and organization-serving. Let's compare this to a different but real world example so we can better understand it. In 1833, William Forster Lloyd published a pamphlet describing the overgrazing of public land, or a "common." Hypothetically, if the cattle herders having access to the common continued to add more cattle, the common would deplete itself. Self-interest would destroy the communities' resources necessary for sustainability.

Volunteers are vital investors. How many volunteers sign-up for an organization, hoping they can make a difference? How many volunteers become disillusioned when organizations forget, ignore, or push them through orientation because there is no strategy for volunteer influx or there are poorly designed roles? How many volunteers quit and then resolve to not volunteer again based on one bad experience? This is volunteer depletion.

Volunteers are not re-seeding themselves. Poor experiences don't cause them to shrug it off, look elsewhere and invite their friends to join them in the struggle.

And so unwittingly, we are depleting the volunteer common. We cling to our volunteers. We clutch them in an outmoded retention model. We are advised that if we simply acknowledge them or cheerfully communicate with them or give them an award, they will stay. We try to retain volunteers on our outdated volunteer management conveyor belt.

We know volunteers are talented and want meaningful roles. What if we don't have one available for them? Do we use a bait and switch method and railroad them into another role we feel pressured to fill? Do we ask them to wait for their desired job to come open? Do we shake our heads at the waste because we know our organizations aren't interested in using their skill-set for something new? Do we hope the volunteer will feel guilty and want to contribute in the ways we've outlined?

We are experts at looking out for our volunteers even though we are working within a system that hinders us. But what if we had free rein with our volunteers and could put their needs ahead of ours, what would we do?

We could take volunteer engagement a step further and look at volunteering from a volunteer's perspective instead of putting organizational needs first. We could admit we don't have volunteers' best interest at heart, not completely anyway.

What if we admitted that although we excel at inspiring and motivating our volunteers, our organizations' needs keep us hamstrung and stuck herding volunteers into pre-designed roles? And by our dedication to meet the needs of our organizations, we inadvertently contribute to a **volunteer talent churn**, one which keeps us looking to replenish volunteers. Sadly, if the nonprofit world continues to ignore the changing volunteer landscape, we will see depleting retention practices dry up our volunteer investors.

So, what can we do to reframe volunteer retention as volunteer sustainability? Let's begin by looking at volunteers as human capital we can cultivate, nourish and sustain. What would this system look like?

Step 5 is creating a movement in volunteer sustainability. As volunteer managers move into organizational leadership in thought and action, the logical next step is to become leaders of a movement in sustainability. Sustainable volunteering will inspire our organizations to rethink outmoded hoarding of precious resources and move towards a model putting the community of volunteers first to reseed them.

A real world example of depletion and sustainability is the practice of crop rotation. Farmers who planted the same crop year after year found that repeated plantings depleted soil nutrients necessary for growth. By rotating plantings on a two-or three-year cycle, soil nutrients replenished. Instead of gobbling up more land to deplete, farmers learned that adjusting for soil requirements solved the problem. Farms became sustainable. What are our volunteer sustainability soil requirements?

Step 5 is seeking alliances for sustainability. Engaging volunteers in silos leads to depletion. Remember back in step 3, distancing yourself from your organization's structure to unleash your role as an entrepreneur of volunteer assets?

Stepping outside the organizational confines gives you a clearer vision. It not only allows you to view your role with more clarity, it detaches volunteering from the organizational host body. Where, now that you have detached it, can you find the lifeblood to sustain it?

As an ecosystem of living, breathing volunteers, how can we give volunteers the nourishment that makes them healthy? While many volunteers flourish under an organizational host body, many others wither and die.

It is the volunteers who wither under the outdated volunteer management system that can be cultivated to grow outside the host organization. Where do we get the nutrients to help them grow? Partnerships with other volunteer managers is key to creating a sustainable volunteer common. Volunteer manager peer groups are the perfect place to begin.

Typically, peer group meetings disseminate information on the latest trends in management, share invitations to recruitment fairs, and lead discussions on shared challenges. Local volunteer manager associations are not places in which a volunteer manager would borrow a volunteer from another organization, but what if they were?

Let's envision a web designer Ali approaches an organization and wants to volunteer his services. If the organization is a well-established one, they most likely have already paid for web design services and will turn Ali away after offering him an alternative role, one he may or may not try. Let's speculate he doesn't want to do anything but web design. Ali must then go about finding another organization needing his services. He may be savvy in how to look for volunteer opportunities, but how much time will he spend and what about the potential volunteer who is not savvy? Does that volunteer give up or will he scour the internet or ask friends or make phone calls?

In a **volunteer sustainability model**, each organization within a community would share their needs with one other and would *match a potential volunteer to the organization and role most closely meeting the needs of the volunteer instead of the volunteer just meeting the needs of the organization.*

We would match volunteers beyond the doors and opportunities within the organization they approached. We would also share volunteers. Let's generate a fictitious volunteer, Lara. Lara has mad marketing skills. She approaches an organization who engages her as a volunteer consultant. Lara is instrumental in constructing a very successful donor campaign.

While that campaign is ongoing, there is a lull in work but Lara is still in success mode and ready to do more. Unfortunately, she has to wait to volunteer her expertise until the next campaign begins. Her enthusiasm cools as she waits for another call. By the time her organization contacts her, she's moved on. Maybe she'll contact her organization down the road, or find another, and maybe she won't. Underutilization has depleted Lara's connection and impetus to continue.

But let's visualize under a **volunteer sustainability model**, Lara has just finished her stint creating the successful donor campaign. Since Lara's enthusiasm is still high, her volunteer manager realizes it will be awhile before marketing calls on Lara's talents again, so he lends her out to a start-up mission.

The start-up desperately needs Lara's skills. She significantly impacts their ability to grow. Results are staggering. Lara continues to volunteer at that mission and helps them realize their potential. Is this a bad thing because she left her original organization? No, quite the opposite and this is why:

- Lara's potential is encouraged, not shelved.
- Lara's skills increase.
- Lara is grateful to her original organization for helping her unleash her passion and will forever advocate for that organization. She is a true supporter.
- Lara keeps her level of volunteering enthusiasm going and when asked to help with the next campaign at her original organization, she will be more likely to say yes.
- The community benefits greatly from Lara's passion and expertise.
- Lara will recruit more volunteers through social media, friends and business associates for both organizations.
- The start-up mission will refer volunteers to Lara's original organization and vice versa.
- A partnership between the two organizations will lead to better use of resources.
- Word will spread about the unselfish alliance and support for both organizations will increase.
- Established volunteers will applaud the gesture.

Larger, more established organizations have more resources. Potential volunteers often gravitate towards the larger organizations because of name recognition or financially positioned recruitment techniques or more press coverage. It takes word of mouth or extensive research for a volunteer to find volunteer opportunities. It doesn't have to be hard if we use our contacts with other volunteer managers to help.

Other, less established organizations miss out on the volunteer who could help them. Volunteer managers at the larger organizations are mostly unaware of these smaller organization's needs and are unwittingly shelving the volunteers that would thrive at a start-up. This is unintentional volunteer hoarding and depletion.

There's another issue at play. The larger and more established an organization becomes, the more risk management invades every aspect of operation, including volunteer services. Volunteer roles become tightened. Volunteers are not allowed to freely use their judgment. Liability shadows every decision. Volunteer rules and policies grow, thick and cumbersome. The volunteers who love the freedom of pioneering new concepts feel choked at more restrictive organizations. Referring these pioneer volunteers to a start-up where they can put their enthusiasm to use is putting the volunteer's needs ahead of organizational constrictions.

But wait. Organizations compete for resources. They compete for donations, grant money, press coverage, celebrity endorsements, in-kind donations, great staff members, space and volunteers. Why should we share volunteers?

Step 5 is putting volunteering influencers ahead of organizational constraints. We know volunteering is an ecosystem. No volunteer exists in a vacuum, i.e., no volunteer exists without the factors making up their experience. Volunteer managers know this and all these ancillary factors swirl around each volunteer and influence their decision to engage or leave.

These influencers make up the ecosystem and sustainable volunteering takes into consideration the ecosystem and its delicate balance. What are the influences that govern whether a volunteer continues to volunteer? There are hundreds, maybe thousands that include personal circumstances, treatment when volunteering, role fit, as well as satisfaction with tasks, recognition and more.

What influencers can we control? What influencers can we tweak? And what influencers do we have no control over? In agriculture, a farmer cannot control whether a tornado will strike his crops. Similarly, in volunteerism, we can't control whether a volunteer falls ill or loses a job or can no longer drive. However, those life altering influencers may be the one reason a volunteer stops volunteering and we must regretfully let the volunteer go with an invitation to return when they are able. We would label those life circumstances as having to "accept."

What about the influencers we can exert control over or can tweak? These are the ones that encourage sustainable growth.

Step 5 is strategizing the volunteer influencers we can control and tweak. In step 2 we discussed the needs of the modern volunteer and those needs are the influencers we can exert control over or at least tweak to increase volunteer sustainability. While we can't control whether a volunteer moves away, we can control the time it takes for us to give a prospective volunteer a callback. While we may not control every volunteer request, we can exert our leadership from all the previous steps to tweak the requests to better fit the needs of today's volunteers.

Let's look at matching volunteers to roles, timely placement and impact. How can we tweak them so volunteers are better served? In a **volunteer sustainability model**, we can partner with other volunteer organizations to meet the needs of our volunteers. If we share a volunteer more suited to another organization with them, wouldn't they want to share a better match with us? And wouldn't the shared volunteers' satisfaction increase and wouldn't they want to keep volunteering?

We know volunteers talk. They share their experiences, whether positive or negative with their families, friends and neighbors, especially on social media. We can safely assume the more satisfied a volunteer is, the more positive messaging they will share.

Let's go back to our volunteer web designer, Ali. When Ali is shelved at a larger organization, what will his message be to his circle of family and friends? Will he say, "Don't bother, they have nothing for you to do?" But if the organization who can't use Ali's specialized skill set refers him to another who desperately needs web design, how will Ali's view of volunteering change and what will he say to others not only about volunteering, but about the organization putting his needs above their own?

When hearing organizations are committed to finding the best fit for them, people hesitant about volunteering will be encouraged to give it a try. And isn't this a powerful message creating further positive ramifications with donors, grant funders and the community?

When attending volunteer manager peer group meetings, share your volunteer needs with one another. Ask if anyone has underutilized (shelved) volunteers and look for ways in which to engage them in other capacities. Treating other organizations as partners, not competitors when engaging volunteers nourishes sustainability for all.

Step 5 is bringing the benefits of volunteering out of the shadows and into the light. Every day, volunteer managers witness the tangible rewards their volunteers reap from volunteering. Beyond "giving back" lies the many secondary byproduct benefits volunteers receive from their volunteer experience; benefits we can record and share.

There are many studies suggesting volunteering aids in well-being, but isn't well-being another obscure concept? If we break well-being down into concrete metrics, we see the various tangible areas represented. Some secondary byproduct volunteering areas include:

•Helping unemployed people fill in gaps in their resumes and offering recommendations from organizational staff.

•Giving students service learning opportunities and organizational recommendations when they seek entry into the college of their choice.

- Giving corporate teams a chance to learn new skills and connect with each other.
- Partnering with corporations to aid in work/life balance.
- Helping people learn about inter-generational connections or diversity because of a pairing with someone different from them.
- Giving isolated individuals a chance to socialize and connect, thus decreasing their risk for illness and depression.
- Putting retired people on the path to a volunteering career and helping them stay active with meaningful work.
- Giving seniors a place to use their skills, a recommended method to ward off dementia and Alzheimer's.
- Creating the citizens of the future due to skills sharpened, such as philanthropy and leadership.
- Helping integrate exchange students and other foreign visitors to our country.
- Opportunities for participating in shared visions.

This under reported phenomena is akin to grow lights and plant food in sustaining volunteerism. We have this amazing information in our toolbox. Although we talk about the benefits of volunteering, we don't shape it into a metric tool. It's time to measure volunteering byproducts for two purposes: Explaining volunteer engagement and highlighting community benefits.

Shed light on the benefits of volunteering to strengthen your argument for meaningful volunteer roles and point to sustaining your volunteer team. You can at first call it a **volunteer retention report** instead of a **volunteer sustainability report** to use verbiage that makes it more easily understood, but we need to move away from calling the sustaining of volunteers "retention." Remember gathering your volunteers' goals and motivations through goal setting in step 4?

Use these goals and motivations when reporting on successful volunteer stories and make the connection between how our volunteers view their volunteering with the volunteer synergy that occurs when their motivations and goals are met. This synergy is the foundation for sustainable volunteering.

Once again, surveys and testimonials are key to measuring data viewed as difficult to capture. Harvest these secondary byproducts of volunteering from survey questions or stories of volunteers who benefited personally through their volunteering. It may seem burdensome having to capture all this data, but it is worth it.

When we ask volunteers about their experience, they feel our commitment to making their volunteering meaningful. When we inform volunteers of the impact they make, they understand their value.

Our phones have note keeping apps, so jot short notes when you hear anecdotal stories your volunteers share. Capture data at meetings or on sign-in sheets. Within these stories is the supporting evidence you need to show volunteer synergy. As you become accustomed to saving evidence, capturing it becomes easier.

Step 5 is quantifying volunteering's benefits. Call it a **Community Benefit Report** and show how volunteering enhances the lives of your community's residents. Offer it as an addendum to a grant proposal, or the subject of a news story, or share it with your local government. By all means, use it as a recruitment tool. It sets your organization apart as one recognizing the importance of the well-being of the community beyond the mission. It becomes a part of a CSR or more accurately, an **OSR**, an **organizational social responsibility**.

Step 5 is partnering with other volunteer organizations to strengthen the volunteerism ecosystem. Sharing volunteers is just one way to control influencers. There are other ways that benefit each volunteer program. Band together to pool resources. Remember how important continuous volunteer education is to volunteers? Instead of working in silos where each volunteer manager struggles to come up with educational offerings two or three times a year for their volunteers, connect with other volunteer managers and share the responsibility.

Ask each volunteer manager to concentrate on one educational seminar and invite volunteers from every organization in your area. Concentrating on one educational offering a year allows each volunteer manager in charge to put all their effort into one seminar, thus increasing its excellence. Multiply all the concentrated creativity by the number of participating managers. That's a lot of great content.

Encourage your volunteers to mingle at shared events. Let their enthusiasm convince each other to volunteer more. Meet volunteers from partner organizations. Pool your budgets and splurge on a featured speaker for yourselves or your volunteers.

Step 5 is strengthening each leader of volunteers. Share more than volunteers and resources. Share best practices with your fellow volunteer managers. Help each other become excellent **leaders of volunteer engagement and impact** so that every member of the community volunteer pool has a meaningful and satisfying experience no matter which organization they volunteer for. The goal is to organize a network of great volunteer organizations so that volunteers in your community want to continue and increase their volunteering.

Can you think back to a time when a new volunteer came to you because they had moved to your area? If they had volunteered at another organization they came, deeply influenced by the methods their previous volunteer manager used. Some of these volunteers integrated beautifully, and you wanted to thank the volunteer manager who cultivated them. Others had developed bad habits and now you had to break them. The more we help one another and elevate our volunteer management skills, the better it is for all volunteer organizations and volunteerism.

Mentor one another. Seek expert advice and share it with your peers. Subscribe to newsletters and websites and discuss techniques at meetings.

Pool your money and share a webinar or send one of your members to a conference with the promise they will bring back the latest in volunteer management techniques. Create a united front of professional management so your community is an example of the best practices in volunteering.

Step 5 is strengthening your leadership in improving your community. Don't keep your partnerships hidden and be afraid to trumpet your sustainability success. Show your respective organizations the knowledge, resources, support, new ideas and inspiration you share with one another.

It may just spur your organization to embrace the benefits of sustainability and apply it to other areas. Your volunteer engagement and impact program can lead the way into a future where missions sustain themselves by cultivating resources, partnering and putting community needs ahead of hoarding and depletion.

Step 5 is treating volunteers realistically and preparing them for service. Sometimes we can feel as though we are recruiting volunteers through a sieve. We bring them in and they filter out and then we must recruit more volunteers to replace them. Then, because we grow tired of the never ending **volunteer talent churn**, we end up fussing over new volunteers, desperate to make their experiences good enough to keep them.

We agonize over placing volunteers into the departments that request them and like helicopter parents, we constantly hover overhead. We know overworked and stressed staff will not cocoon volunteers the way we did when we conducted orientation or interviewed them and we think back to the way we assured the new volunteer they would be part of a caring team.

So, we follow the new volunteer around, smoothing rough patches, acting as a go-between and insulating them from harsh realities. The truth is, sustainability does not come from Band-Aid practices.

At some point, a hovered over volunteer will run into a sticky situation. What if you are unavailable? Volunteer sustainability entails more than creating a volunteer friendly atmosphere. It calls for realistic volunteer expectations.

Our role in readying the volunteer for service involves mentoring, coaching, encouraging and investing in that volunteer. Staff doesn't have the time nor energy to keep up the same level of encouragement and investment. So, what can we do about this disconnect?

Two things:

The first is devising a **new volunteer integration plan**: Prior to placing volunteers within a department, work with the department to plan how the volunteer will integrate. A few areas of planning include answering these questions:

- Who will oversee the volunteer: A specific person, a person of the day or a variety of people?
- Who is the point person to answer volunteer questions and who is the ultimate authority over the task?
- What are the procedures for calling out sick, coming in late?
- Who will review the volunteer and on what basis?
- What is the recourse for volunteer problems and challenges?

Remind staff you are there to help not only the volunteer, but to help staff as well and you will listen to and work towards a solution for any problem staff is experiencing. If we want staff's buy-in, we must take into consideration their feelings before, during and after we assign a volunteer to them.

Listening to staff expectations before placing a volunteer helps us prepare the volunteer to work with specific staff. Checking in periodically helps us intercept any problems before they grow and surveying staff after a volunteer leaves helps us in matching future volunteers to department personalities.

The second strategy is **ready the volunteer for the real world**: Volunteer managers can inadvertently establish a sense of bubble-wrapping volunteers by extensive coaching and by stroking a volunteer's ego and sense of importance.

I don't mean we should never make our volunteers feel important, but we must realize that the more we make everything about the volunteer, the greater the shock will be when they arrive for their volunteer job and find that staff won't baby them.

Instead, we must carefully prepare volunteers for the reality that departments and staff will not continue the coddling, but rather, will expect supportive work. If staff have to spend more time stroking a volunteer's ego than the volunteer accomplishes, staff will reject volunteers altogether and volunteers will quit because reality did not meet their expectations.

We must not expect staff to socialize, to listen to endless stories, to bolster spirits or to care more about the volunteer than their work. In the beginning, a volunteer has to prove their worth by helping, not distracting and we must prepare them for this reality. It is backwards to expect staff to forge a relationship with a volunteer simply because the volunteer has a good heart. Relationships with staff will grow, but only after the volunteer has proven themselves and contributed, not before.

How do we prepare volunteers for the real world of volunteering? Ease them from cocooning. Stress from day one, the importance of the mission. We can still coach and mentor them, but we must integrate the message of expectations.

A leader of volunteers who can coach and mentor a volunteer to succeed is one who balances messaging. The agile leader looks for the strengths in volunteers and reinforces and guides those strengths towards accomplishing mission goals. The volunteer will be better prepared to integrate into working alongside staff when we encourage them to use their strengths and not fall back on weaknesses. Volunteers who are mentored in expectations will be less likely to leave when hand-holding ends.

But let's go back for a minute, to internal volunteer retention. How do businesses predict the loss of customers? How do we keep our existing volunteers from leaving and send us into a **volunteer talent churn**?

While we can't do much about life circumstances that force volunteers to quit, there are four categories defining a disenfranchised volunteer at a high risk for quitting.

The categories are:

Volunteer attrition due to an event: Something happened to disappoint or anger the volunteer.

Volunteer attrition due to fading away: The volunteer doesn't hold the same passion about volunteering and is slowly moving away.

Volunteer attrition due to underutilization: The volunteer feels as though his/her skills are not being put to adequate use.

Volunteer attrition due to the inability to find a fit: The volunteer's experience does not match his/her expectations or a volunteer does not mesh with the work.

While each volunteer is unique, we can learn from and apply the underlying reasons disenfranchised volunteers leave us. An exit interview is essential if you can contact the volunteer. Often volunteers stop answering our calls and emails without informing us why. It's frustrating, so it's important to conduct a **stay interview** to help catch problems before the volunteer quits.

Always give volunteers permission to step away. If volunteers feel guilty about "quitting," the likelihood they will return some day is slim. But, when they feel acceptance in their decision to step away, they will be more likely to return at some point.

I'll never forget walking to my office one day and seeing a former volunteer sitting in the lobby. "I told you I would come back," she said after being gone for 8 years.

In our volunteer sustainability model, offer to connect a volunteer who is thinking of leaving to other organizations. Reinforce the volunteer's talents and contributions to your program while projecting their future success at another organization and encourage them to continue volunteering, even if it means their departure. Sometimes sustainability comprises letting go so the volunteer can continue to grow.

Let's revisit Jazmine's story at the beginning of step 5. She said she loves the organization, so why is she thinking of quitting? We can eliminate volunteer attrition due to an event. But, what about volunteer attrition due to fading away? She says she's not enjoying her job anymore. But she feels pressured to keep grinding away at it.

We can also blame volunteer attrition due to underutilization. Jazmine wants to use her new specialized skills, something she is passionate about, but was told it wasn't an option.

We could also lump in volunteer attrition due to inability to find a fit. It's not just new volunteers who may experience challenges in finding the right fit for them. Existing good volunteers like Jazmine can also want to use different or new skills and keeping them in a task box is even more destructive when it results in losing an already engaged volunteer.

Analyze the reasons volunteers leave from exit interviews. Do one or more of the attrition reasons form a pattern? If most volunteers leave because they are under-utilized, then sustainability calls for advocating for more meaningful roles for volunteers.

This may work in some organizations, and may be more challenging in others. Let's go back again to the **Goal Setting** report that placed expectations for the next year against results in step 4. Cause and effect is a powerful tool when backed up by actual statistics from volunteer surveys and interviews.

On the flip side, gather information from your key volunteers. What is it that motivates them? What do they enjoy most about their volunteering experience? Use their input to attract more volunteers like them. Develop targeted recruitment strategies using key volunteers' input. Change your recruitment ads frequently and track the ads producing the most interest.

Step 5 is following up on volunteer motivations. Just acknowledging our volunteers' motivations is not enough. **Volunteer motivation investment** means revisiting volunteer motivations and goals to ensure they are being met.

At the annual review and goal setting from step 4, we ask volunteers to outline their mission objectives for the coming year. But maybe there's more to volunteer goals than just mission goals.

What about the volunteer on a personal level? When a new volunteer comes onboard, ask them to list **personal volunteering goals**, such as learning a new skill, meeting new people or paying an organization back for services rendered. This insight is a window into volunteer sustainability.

Secondary reasons for volunteering get at the heart of the volunteer's motivations beyond helping. By revisiting goals after a few months to see if both personal and mission goals are being met, we are reinforcing the motivations for volunteering.

This method of investing in volunteer motivation can also extend to corporate partnerships and episodic groups. When engaging with a group, follow up with more than a thank-you letter. Include a simple questionnaire asking how the volunteer experience benefited the group's members.

Include questions that ask, "How can we do better next time?" Besides gathering valuable feedback, you are sending the message you care about the group's time and efforts and sincerely want to see them derive tangible benefits from the time spent with your organization. Again, this is another source of impact reporting metrics.

Our underlying partnership goal is not to accomplish a one day task, but to forge **volunteering partnerships** with individuals and groups. A partnership by definition is never one sided. Sustainable volunteering comes from partnering with those who volunteer. For individuals, our partnership comprises everything we've outlined so far in volunteer engagement. It is our investment in the individual volunteer that makes us good partners.

Let's look at a **corporate volunteer partner**. If we convey to them a message that says, "Your business should support us because we do good work," or if we take and take, then we can't call it a partnership.

Instead, strive for an equal partner volunteer/business relationships. Equal partnerships involve giving and getting on both sides. For your corporate partners:

Balance mission impact with employee skills sharpening and leadership training. Balance mission awareness with employee morale improvement. Balance increased company involvement with organizational newsletter recognition. Show your commitment to a corporate volunteering initiative that also benefits the businesses who volunteer. Document and share the balancing benefits with your corporate partner.

Step 5 is the cultivation of organic volunteering. Remember in step 2, the citizen helpers who are those new and modern volunteers who just might leave us behind as they seek pure, unfiltered volunteering experiences? Leaders of volunteers have a ground floor opportunity here to help sustain citizen helpers.

How many of these **organic volunteer pods** are out there? Are they on social sites, calling for help from other concerned citizens? Are they offshoots of parent organizations, or youth sports or conversations on social media about a particular cause?

The citizen helper practices engaged volunteering. Something, somewhere clicked within them and unleashed a desire to put thoughts into action. Offer one of these pods of citizen helpers some volunteer management tips to help them find one another and mobilize.

Think about setting aside one of the national service days and asking your volunteers to help this pod as a service project. As leaders of volunteers, we are by default, **leaders of a sustainable volunteer movement**. This means supporting all forms of volunteering for the common good.

In the United States, Make a Difference Day is a national day of service. I would ask our volunteers to join me on that day in helping a struggling organization accomplish a goal. The response was always positive, and it created goodwill and awareness for our organization. We won a state award for our outreach.

The thing about outreach is the people we helped through volunteering for a completely unrelated mission are people who could at any moment be served by our mission. Our outreach increased awareness for our organization and the services we provided.

There is an intersection of non-profit missions everywhere. People don't exist in silos. They may need disaster help one day and health-related services another day so the organizations who stop thinking we are competing with one another and instead realize we are all serving our communities are the ones creating sustainability for all.

Find common ground with other causes on social sites. Look for ways their mission intersects with your mission and pilot an initiative to help one another. One example I remember was a local animal shelter allowed my volunteers to "borrow" adoptable animals and bring them to visit with patients.

The patients loved the visits, and family members, staff or volunteers often found a new pet to adopt. A few of my volunteers ended up volunteering for the shelter and we recruited a few shelter volunteers. That's **mission intersection**.

Another way is to offer training via volunteering to volunteers of an unrelated organization. For instance, disaster volunteers can "train" at a health care organization to learn listening skills or at an animal shelter to learn more about pets. Their training through volunteering will increase their effectiveness when deployed to a disaster site and keep them learning while they await an assignment.

Step 5 is working within the growing episodic trend. Instead of trying to force episodic volunteers into recurring roles, encourage volunteers to freestyle. This means adding projects to your traditional roles. Projects are shorter, less rigid and appeal to volunteers who cannot commit. Offer the **freestyle volunteer** the chance to interact with your mission by taking on an independent, outside project.

Outside projects can take many forms, such as research, independent fundraisers and virtual opportunities. Freestylers may try out your organization so introduce them to other possibilities through **exposure to mission impact**.

For example, let's say volunteer Kwan signs up but does not want the scheduled jobs available at your animal shelter, The Ark. Kwan is passionate about helping your no-kill shelter but is hesitant to commit. You offer Kwan a chance to do a pet food drive at his office, which he accepts. He conducts the drive and you then ask him to meet you at the shelter to thank him and accept the donations.

When he arrives, you give him a tour. You, or a key volunteer ask him to feed or walk the cutest dog in the shelter. You immerse him in the mission. After his experience, Kwan might consider an on-call position or might want to come back another day. He may pester his HR specialist at work to put together a corporate volunteer day. If not, you've at least gained a strong supporter.

Let's stop for a moment and examine supporters and the volunteer connection. Take Kwan for example and let's assume he never volunteers at The Ark again. It's a loss, right? No, it's not. Because of his positive experience at The Ark, Kwan:

- Promotes The Ark to his circle of influence as a place to volunteer and donate because he has seen the good work firsthand and was treated with volunteer respect.
- Now considers volunteering a worthwhile venture and will be more likely to volunteer somewhere again.
- Will change his personal behaviors to more closely resemble The Ark's mission (especially if his "tour" includes talking points on "what you can do to help stem unwanted pets from ending up in shelters") and will promote the talking points.
- Will relive the "helper's high" he felt when walking a shelter dog every time he remembers his volunteer experience which increases his wellbeing.
- Will support The Ark in social media.

Go back for a minute to the **volunteer investor**. Once a volunteer leaves, their volunteer experience determines whether they become supporters. In business, research shows that customers are overwhelmingly more likely to share a negative experience than a positive one. And, negative experiences shape customers' future actions. From this we can infer that a negative volunteer experience will:

•Cause the volunteer to share a negative experience with others.

•Keep the volunteer from supporting by donating/volunteering/advocating in the future.

It is imperative we ensure positive volunteering experiences, even if they are one-time or episodic, because experiences determine if one-time volunteers become supporters. Garnering positive support is much more difficult than creating negative non-support.

Each episodic volunteer is important because organizational supporters exponentially grow mission reach and influence. And, in a volunteer sustainability model, each volunteer who has a positive experience will reseed.

But let's stop here for a moment. What if we looked at creating supporters after a person volunteers as a backwards goal? Why don't we create supporters from the start? We strive to make our volunteers feel a part of the mission through our processes, but we can make everyone, even those who do not follow through on volunteering feel part of our missions. How?

Label each person who inquires as a supporter or advocate. In orientation or at an open house for potential volunteers, welcome people to your organization by calling them **advocates for the mission**. Even if they don't volunteer, whether by your choice or theirs, they can still be supporters. Include them in emails, invitations to events. Make advocating for your organization about action with **volunteering an elevated form of advocacy**. Make them understand that they are now part of your organization by calling them advocates and encourage them to apply to boost their advocacy by becoming volunteers.

Enlisting potential volunteers as advocates upfront accomplishes two things: The first is obvious. It adds action to the potential volunteer's inquiry into your organization. Equip the new advocate with talking points, donation information and show them how to promote your mission. They will talk anyway, so let's give them the proper way to present mission work and make them feel part of something in motion.

The second accomplishment is in elevating volunteerism. Make volunteering for your organization an elevated form of advocacy, one that advocates would want to aspire to. This sets the tone that volunteering for your mission is serious and that not just any warm body will do. It allows you to present your policies and procedures as part of the step up into volunteering.

Step 5 is streamlining the volunteering process and ramping up exposure to mission impact. Offer a trial basis for hard to fill jobs, or exploratory volunteer opportunities that do not involve commitment. For those potential volunteers who are hesitant or feel inadequate or unsure, signing up for a commitment can be overwhelming.

Too many choices is also daunting and the volunteer may feel as though they have no idea where they fit. Give them the chance to try a volunteer position with no strings attached. If they cannot find a suitable fit, ask them to continue their advocacy and keep an eye out for any friends or family who might be perfect for the job. Treating them with respect for their time keeps them supporting and advocating.

Build a **volunteer mentoring tour** that allows new volunteers to experience many roles. Partner with your volunteer manager peer group to offer students a chance to rotate volunteering assignments during summer break. Research shows that exposure to volunteering early creates future volunteers. Think long-term and along with your volunteer manager peers, present a variety of volunteering opportunities to middle and high school students.

Step 5 is using terms to mobilize. Mobilized citizens are a fearsome force. The nature of their independence may pose a barrier to fitting them into a traditional role, but they can be supportive in helpful ways.

They can advise on the use of social media and help get your message out, especially if your mission compliments the work being done by the volunteer pod.

Pod members can think of ways to tackle issues such as diversity, inclusion and acceptance. Their passionate involvement in the cause they champion can lead you to resources that help your program embrace change.

A word of caution though with volunteers passionate about politics or religion or other possibly polarizing stances. Their motivation to volunteer may center on spreading a message and convincing others to think the way they think. That motivation goes against the basic tenets of most modern organizations that have no religious or political basis. Volunteers whose main reason to volunteer is to further their ideology will nearly always default to spreading the word about their beliefs, even after agreeing to remain neutral.

Organic movements may seem opposite our structured, more formal volunteering model, but they share the desire to be **change agents.** Borrow the verbiage these organic movements use and recruit volunteers to your organization with the urgency appealing to citizen helpers.

Terms to borrow include:
- Calls to action.
- Change agents.
- Raising awareness.
- Stopping (insert your mission's goal here) now.
- Mobilizing.
- Activism.
- Advocacy.

These terms speak to results. Often, volunteer recruitment ads sound more like 9-5 jobs, instead of initiatives moving toward a solution. Recurring positions often sound tedious and don't appeal to today's more results-oriented volunteers.

Instead of making every volunteer position sound like a lifelong commitment, design roles with a defined end. Make them part of a volunteer project having actionable results to attract modern volunteers. Let's say for instance, your health-related volunteer organization cares for people with a specific disease. You may advertise for patient care volunteers.

Since there is no foreseeable end to the need for patient care volunteers until there is a cure, this volunteer position sounds like a long-term commitment, which can discourage volunteers who aren't interested in or don't know if they want to stay long-term.

Break the timeframe down into a smaller piece with an actionable end by advertising for patient care volunteers to "eliminate patient isolation by the end of this year." Be prepared to measure the percentage by which volunteering reduces patient isolation so you can present the statistics to your volunteers. Help them understand that they accomplished a goal and hopefully they will stay longer for the new goal you establish for the following year.

Modern volunteers crave action and results. Political volunteering meets these needs. Volunteers mobilize (canvas) and see results (election). There is a defined action and an end. Think about your volunteer opportunities and how you can rework them to meet actions and results.

This doesn't mean using a bait and switch tactic or hiding a recurring role behind new language. Instead, honestly rework roles to include both recurring ways of volunteering and action/results ways of volunteering.

Speaking of recruitment, take a step back and look at your workspace or office. Is it filled with family photos, inspirational sayings and knick-knacks volunteers have given you over the years?

While cute decorations may feel comforting, they don't represent your **volunteer engagement and impact brand.** Treat your office as a visual recruitment tool. A volunteer storyboard, printed testimonials and photos of volunteers at work say to a prospective volunteer, "Here, in this place, volunteers are at work to make a real difference."

Other ways to embrace organically sustainable volunteering are:

Invest in your partnerships with other volunteer managers to develop a **volunteering campaign** call to action to benefit both missions. Encourage comments from volunteers and members of the community who will applaud you for your innovative movement and then use those comments to bolster your **leadership value**.

Devise projects allowing volunteers to work outside the organization on their own. Think outside the traditional box and craft initiatives that impact awareness or inclusion or community benefits. Watch for successful campaigns, borrow the methods that worked and apply them to your mission goals.

One project I developed was a fun usage of social media. A volunteer who owned a therapy dog Gabby, was an excellent writer. She would journal her visits to patients in nursing homes and share the entries with me.

I asked her to post stories on our volunteer page but from Gabby's perspective and she agreed. The stories of therapy dog Gabby's adventures and his sensitive "take" on the humans he visited took on a whole new life and reached a larger audience. His posts invited the people who read them to think of volunteering in a whole new way.

Step 5 is embracing mission centric expectations. Don't be afraid to put responsibility onto volunteers. I remember a highly skilled volunteer, Gwen. I called her many times, but she always had an excuse for not getting started. I emailed her, invited her to functions, sent her information and in reality, chased her. It frustrated me that I couldn't convince her to come in.

I noticed that every volunteer I spent a great deal of time chasing usually faded away rather quickly. The point is, we can't make people volunteer. We can't make people do a good job because we are nice, or we listen endlessly or we care.

If we want quality volunteers, then we must lay out expectations. We expect volunteers to be on time, especially if they work with vulnerable populations. We expect volunteers to follow the rules. We expect volunteers to turn in documentation. We expect quality because our clients deserve nothing less.

Expecting quality is not the antithesis of mentoring and coaching; in fact the opposite is true. Think of sports movies about teams that overcame odds. The coach instilled excellence in these teams. Encouraging quality is the basis for mentoring and coaching. If we are fine with mediocrity, then we will get mediocrity. Instead, if we coach a person to be the best version of themselves, then we will have quality volunteers.

Weave organizational expectations into interactions with volunteers, especially new or potential volunteers. When interviewing new volunteers, immediately equate their personalities, talents and skills to the ways they will use those skills to further organizational goals.

More than policies and procedures which target conduct, expectations revolve around volunteer contributions and the bringing of their best. It is a compliment to volunteers when we expect great things from them. Lowering expectations sends the message we think little of volunteers, and we think less of their contributions.

The desire to produce exceptional work will attract volunteers, not repel them. Who doesn't want to be part of an exceptional team? This doesn't mean we expect perfection. There is an enormous difference between quality and perfection. When speaking to volunteers, refer to quality as being the best version of themselves. Sure, we make mistakes and we are not perfect. Our clients don't expect perfection, but they do desire authenticity and sincerity.

Refer to the expectations right from the get go, starting with orientation. In the past, we groveled at volunteer orientation, gushing to new volunteers, "We are just so grateful you are here."

Groveling doesn't instill confidence but the notion that quality pervades everything we do will inspire it. Make volunteers feel as though they are the cream of the crop. The expectation of quality volunteering lends credence to rules and policies, making it understandable to enforce requirements and helps tremendously when having to counsel a volunteer who has erred.

Establish volunteering as a next step advocacy position. Enlist people who inquire about volunteering as advocates first, then introduce the policies, procedures and qualifications surrounding volunteering.

Go over expectations and rules. Make volunteering something to aspire to and reinforce how volunteering is a privilege. The upfront expectation of quality helps when having to turn a potential volunteer down for an assignment.

Step 5 is recognizing the need for change management:
Change is difficult, and change can come from many directions. It can result from the fluid movement of organic volunteer ecosystems or it could be a change within your organizational structure impacting policies or roles or initiatives. Often senior administrations structure changes in policy behind closed doors and then unveil the changes to the volunteer manager without warning or input.

Many volunteer managers have experienced a "volunteer mutiny" when changes are unexpectedly implemented. Volunteers can revolt, or leave in mass, not necessarily because of the change itself, but because of how the change was implemented. Sustaining our volunteers means paying attention to how change affects them, being willing to work with them and encouraging their feedback.

Savvy volunteer managers know from experience the successful implementation of change is not announcing to the volunteers, "We have a new policy." Instead, the volunteer manager incorporates the tenets of **volunteer change management**, which are:

• Impacted stakeholders: Determine who is impacted by the change-all volunteers, some volunteers, future volunteers, staff, and/or clients.

• Explanation period: Open a back and forth dialogue with the volunteers. Explain the why and be gracious and committed to effective mediation when receiving complaints. Reframe from grumbling that you don't agree with the change.

Assure the volunteers your organization and you appreciate their cooperation. Reiterate the mission is still front and center. Ask a member of senior management to come to a volunteer meeting to explain. If they are unable, ask a member of administration to pen a letter praising the volunteers for their continued support and read that letter to them.

• Pilot projects: Choose several volunteers to pilot the change to work out the bugs, or understand future objections and/or questions.

• Feedback: Continue to gather feedback so volunteer input is heard and respected. Advocate for a fluid change to incorporate volunteer suggestions.

• Rollout: Introduce the change under an announced rollout and continue dialogue and feedback.

Helping volunteers embrace change from the start through a **change management strategy** will set the stage for a smoother transition. Reassure volunteers that their voices will be heard and their concerns given consideration.

Change is inevitable but pushing changes onto volunteers without a **change management strategy** doesn't have to be. Ask upper management to give you ample time before starting changes so you can prepare volunteers. Explain that change transitions are smoother when volunteers are prepared and not expected to adapt to change when it happens.

If they don't and drop a change onto your plate, diplomatically inform them you will begin your change management strategy but it will take time to implement. Share volunteer feedback, not as a "see I told you this would be hard," but rather as an illustration of the need for change management strategies.

Step 5 is practicing organic volunteer leadership. Organic leadership comes from the observation of nature, and how systems naturally evolve and survive. Volunteer management is like a complex ecosystem. Let's look at a pond in very simplistic terms. A pond is comprising water, minerals, sunlight, aquatic plants, living creatures, decomposers, animals that feed on the pond occupants and more. Each component influences the others and contributes to the overall system.

Volunteer management is a complex ecosystem. We talked about the influencers you can control versus the ones you have to accept and the ones in between that you can tweak. The "tweak-able" influencers will be the bulk of your influencers that are fluid, but can offer some amazing opportunities to design a **volunteer engagement and impact program** that is innovative and successful.

Try this exercise: Take time, find a quiet place and bring a piece of blank paper. Draw a circle in the middle and label it volunteer engagement and impact. Now surround the circle with any and every factor you can think of that influences a volunteer's engagement and impact.

Influencers can be positive or negative such as 'distance from the volunteering site,' or 'staff treatment on the volunteer's first day' or 'lack of proper training.' Draw a line from the volunteer engagement and impact circle to each influencer.

It won't take you long to have thirty or forty influencers on the page. Lean back and look for any connections between influencers and draw lines connecting them. Influencers such as volunteer skills connect with roles available. Now label each influencer as either "control," or "tweak," or "accept."

While we cannot physically move a volunteer's house closer to our office (we have to label this as accept), we might offer a new role done from home (which could move it into the tweak category). A systems map is a visual aid that helps stimulate creative thinking.

It can also serve as a teaching tool when you are educating staff and administration about volunteer recruitment and retention challenges. Work on your volunteer systems map and look for connections that need work. You can also highlight the connections in order of importance.

You may find you are connecting several influencers to one in particular which means some influencers may act as "umbrellas." Let's say you identify "lack of administration support" as a negative influencer. You have connected "lack of budget," "short orientation," "staff held accountable for volunteer retention," and several others to "lack of administration support," which makes it an umbrella influencer.

This is the reason the visual is so helpful. We can work on each negative influencer separately, or look at the umbrella and plan how to enact a change for the most impact. What steps will I need to take to change a negative umbrella influencer to a positive?

Most volunteer managers are already practicing sustainable organic leadership within their own volunteer programs. Taking volunteer preferences into consideration when assigning tasks is an example of seeing the connection between volunteer talents and preferences and the resulting synergy that meets or exceeds expectations. Being proactive in the 4 previous steps means you are working towards changing negative umbrella influencers to positive ones.

Study your umbrella influencers and look for ways in which you are impacting those influencers. Are you increasing or supporting the positive umbrella influencers or can you do more? On the flip side, what are you doing to change negative umbrella influencers and what new methods can you use for a positive change?

Step 5 is explaining and elevating the complex volunteer ecosystem to the non-profit world by leading up. As the modern leader of volunteers adapts to volunteer needs, assumes a leadership role, sets priorities and vision and implements volunteer sustainability, it is time to lead upwards in organizations. It's time to change the negative umbrella influencers to positive influencers.

Examples of agile organizations and companies point to the methods already employed by most volunteer managers. Volunteer managers are masters at understanding fluidity, are great at implementing agile strategies and are embracing organic coaching and leadership. The problem is, these amazing volunteer managers are not making enough inroads into the senior management level.

What does it mean to lead up?

Participate often and with intent. Speak up in meetings, offer opinions and give insights. Leave the comfort of your office. Mingle with staff, conduct impromptu surveys, talk up your program, personally introduce volunteers, check in with staff working with volunteers, and ask how volunteers can add value. In other words, connect.

Use verbiage supporting your knowledge and expertise. Ditch hedging words so common in volunteer management vocabulary. What are hedging words? Maybe, could be, probably, can vs. will, might, if you want, seemingly and possibly to name just a few.

Any words that do not convey confidence will make everything you say appear wishy-washy. You will find these words appearing everywhere in this book as I am struggling to overcome my many years of using them because I thought they made my communication "nicer." Consider the following two sentences. Which one inspires confidence?

"It's possible our volunteers might potentially help increase donations if we give them training."

"By giving our volunteers the necessary training, donations will increase."

Bring that confident speech when recounting accomplishments and make it specific to enforce the message. Consider these two sentences:

"Our volunteers donated over 200 hours last month in a variety of roles."

"Last month, our volunteer docents impacted 6,000 museum visitors by personalizing their museum visit, disseminating facts in our new exhibit and giving donation information to each visitor. As a result, donations went up last month by 20%."

On the flip side, do not mince words when explaining volunteers don't sit by their phones, or are not willing to do menial tasks. If you look around, you see that those in senior management do not hesitate when explaining their challenges. Don't deliver a message that appears to be your opinion. State facts that you can back up and again, vague wishy-washy words dilute the message. Let's look at these two statements:

"Our volunteers really are not crazy about volunteer of the year awards; they'd rather have something more meaningful."

"Our most recent volunteer poll shows that 48% of volunteers will not attend a volunteer luncheon this year and 98% stated that a volunteer of the year award is outdated. Instead, 92% preferred hearing direct impact statistics in place of awards."

Leading up means having the courage to speak up. Remember, if we act like doormats, everyone will treat us like doormats. But again, explaining challenges leads to the excuse perception, so always temper challenges with alternative solutions. It is the solution-oriented leader of volunteers who will be heard.

Frame your accomplishments in statistics that show measurable results. Advocate for the resources you need, not as a plea, but as a method for furthering the mission and providing excellent, **mission centric volunteer engagement and impact**. Speak the language of progression, improvement and furthering the mission.

Forgo any outdated methods holding you and your initiative back. Instead of money saved, show benefits gained by engaging volunteers. In place of soft words to describe your volunteers, opt for strong words which convey volunteers' skills, professionalism and contributions.

Lessen the attachment to broad emotional terms describing personal attributes like 'heartfelt' and 'giving back' and replace them with results verbs such as impact, change, influence, and affect.

Volunteer sustainability hinges on elevating volunteerism and its impact. It directly links to volunteer satisfaction and meaningful engagement that produces volunteer synergy. It involves embracing a complex volunteer ecosystem, one with fluid connections.

Volunteer sustainability hinges on every volunteer manager's responsibility to reframe **volunteer management as volunteer engagement**, redefine volunteer managers as leaders of volunteers, reshape non-profit culture and re-imagine the future.

We have to remove the obstacles holding us from the respect and inclusion our programs deserve. We cannot look to others to elevate us; we must lift ourselves up. We must disrupt our sense of where we belong in nonprofit hierarchy. It will take a systematic dismantling of the old norm and replacing it with our new normal, one that will provide benefits to our clients, organizations, volunteers and the communities we call home.

When you find you are disrupting the old norm, are committing to volunteer sustainability and are taking the steps to implement mission centric volunteer engagement and impact, then it's on to envisioning the future in step 6.

Step 5 Checklist:
✓ Create a movement in volunteer sustainability
✓ Seek alliances

- ✓ Put volunteering influencers ahead of organizational constraints
- ✓ Strategize volunteer influencers
- ✓ Bring volunteering benefits into the light
- ✓ Quantify volunteering benefits
- ✓ Partner with volunteer organizations to strengthen the volunteer ecosystem
- ✓ Strengthen each leader of volunteers
- ✓ Lead in improving the community
- ✓ Prepare volunteers for realistic service
- ✓ Invest in volunteer motivation
- ✓ Cultivate organic volunteering
- ✓ Work with episodic trends
- ✓ Streamline the process
- ✓ Mobilize
- ✓ Embrace mission centric expectations
- ✓ Understand change management
- ✓ Practice organic leadership
- ✓ Lead up

Step 6: Re-imagining the Future of Volunteer Engagement and Impact

What will volunteerism look like 10 years from now? What about 25, or 30 years? Will leaders of volunteers still have the same conversations, bemoan the same conditions, and argue for the same changes? Will robots take over as roboteers? Will the volunteer management profession die out?

Thankfully, no. Fortunately, volunteering and volunteer management is morphing in an organic and sustainable way. It is adapting to the changing world. People are increasing their compassion and are finding new ways to help.

There are always bumps on the path to change and sometimes it can feel as though the journey to better volunteer engagement and impact is too slow and difficult to make, but ours is a hopeful profession. Heck, we call upon hope every time we engage a volunteer so it's perfectly natural for us to hope for a better future.

Leading volunteers is coming into its own. There is an awakening within our sector. Savvy leaders of volunteers are rejecting the stereotypes surrounding volunteers, volunteerism and volunteer managers and instead, are reshaping themselves and their programs to better meet the challenges of today's society.

All over the world, leaders of volunteers are ushering in cutting-edge ideas out of necessity while they research and learn from successful disciplines unrelated to volunteers.

Courageous leaders of volunteers are finding their voices and banding together to make impactful changes. These brave leaders are disrupting the system and lighting the way.

So, let's fast forward into the future. Imagining future possibilities is not a frivolous exercise. By letting our creative juices flow and conceptualizing a futuristic world, we can awaken innovation and conceive our direction or next initiative.

What will we see in the next 25 to 30 years? Take a moment and envision what volunteering will look like for the next generations. What if volunteering becomes as big as we hope?

Let's have fun and speculate what the future might hold.

Volunteering Gamification: Volunteering is so ingrained into society, it becomes a fun challenge. Fans form fantasy volunteering leagues. Teams vie for online badges and compete with one another. Leveling up comes with measuring impact. Online volunteers trade equipment with each other and a cottage industry pops up surrounding good deeds. Volunteer warrior characters fight evil societal challenges. So, while this is going on, what happens to leaders of volunteers? They become the NPC, the non-player characters guiding the volunteers in their quests.

Volunteer Apps: Volunteering apps include volunteer avatars, hours tracking systems, interactive contests, message boards, forums and more.

Virtual and Micro-volunteering: Virtual volunteering overtakes in-person volunteering. Home visits are replaced with face-to-face software applications. Seniors age in place with the aid of virtual monitoring volunteers. Virtual tutoring helps millions of children worldwide. Virtual advice, from health related to legal gives countless people access to services.

Non-profit Executive Director Requirements: Organizations require potential CEO's or Executive Directors to have volunteer management experience before applying to lead an organization because volunteering is the most important department in an organization(this is my #1 idea of the future). Bonus points for those candidates who did extensive personal volunteering.

Volunteer Course for Elementary Schools: A start-up software developer devises a volunteering platform teaching the benefits of volunteering after a group of volunteer managers pilot a program in their local school district. They follow a group of middle school children as they volunteer. They track the increased self-confidence, grade point average and leadership skills learned and these become the basis for the new program.

These forward-thinking leaders of volunteers devise lesson plans that include projects, leadership initiatives, skills challenges, analyzing data and problem solving. This catches the eye of an educational software firm who launch it world-wide.

Demonization of Donors: Giving money is so yesterday. Donations recede as the primary focus of giving. An organic movement arises taunting "the laziness of just sending in money." The movement champions hands-on involvement while mocking uninvolved donors as "donation clickers" and spreads through social media, causing a pivotal shift in the way community service is viewed. The "I.am.inVOLved" campaign is the new social media darling after a prominent celebrity is photographed volunteering in the I.am.inVOLved shirt.

Activist Volunteer: Activism moves into the mainstream and melds with traditional volunteering. The volunteer activist is a specific role within an organization and the activist volunteers conduct positive protests to spread the word. They are a marketing hybrid that unleashes new methods in reaching goals, outcomes and getting resources.

Organic Volunteering: Volunteers shape their own volunteer experience. Instead of listing volunteer opportunities, organizations list their goals and objectives on volunteer recruitment sites. Potential volunteers read through mission statements and white papers to pick a cause. They then submit their work and hours to the organization for statistical recording.

Multiple Mission Volunteering: Volunteer organizations band together after two creative volunteer managers advertise volunteer opportunities impacting both of their missions.

Volunteers choose from a listings menu combining mission objectives; for example, tutoring a client's children while the client goes to treatment impacts two missions.

The volunteer activity impacts the first mission which ensures patients receive treatment and impacts the second mission, which is to foster literacy in at-risk children. Volunteers gravitate towards multiple mission opportunities. A new theme arises: Making the most impact.

Individual Social Responsibility: Corporate social responsibility gives rise to individual social responsibility. It becomes the top resume enhancer over experience and education and volunteering is the primary source of ISR.

Volunteer Block Chain: Volunteers keep track of their own work and hours in a decentralized system. Hours include helping their elderly neighbor shovel snow, or stopping to help fix a flat tire. Helping others becomes a source of community pride and citizens share hours on community websites. Community leaders use the stats for everything from courting businesses and individuals to move into the community to writing grants and seeking support. The idea catches on and eventually becomes a world-wide phenomenon.

Speed Dating, Volunteer Style: In the spirit of sustainability, volunteer managers band together and host speed dating style volunteer open houses where prospective volunteers can quickly learn about the wide range of volunteering roles available during five-minute interval chats.

Interconnected Volunteering: Global volunteers connect with one another through a website that matches a volunteer with someone who volunteers in a similar role. The website gives the volunteers a platform to share goals and best practices and to support one another. They keep one another volunteering through issuing challenges and comparing notes.

Volunteer Pop-up Shops: Volunteers band together and take over local stores, coffee shops and restaurants for a day. All profits or tips go to local charities.

The Volunteer Pitch Show: Volunteers pitch their organizations to a panel of funders in hopes of securing a grant. Ratings soar after celebrity funders enter the "pitch zone." The show becomes so popular that non-profit funding becomes a staple of every large business. Follow-up episodes track the good work being done by the funding recipient. The businesses who fund the work advertise the impact made by their generous grants.

Live Streaming Volunteering: Volunteering moves from a private and intimate experience to one of public visibility as stigmas surrounding illness, poverty and disaster help lessen and the recipients of volunteer help become more willing to share their stories. Volunteering experiences are some of the most viewed live streaming events and several volunteering channels pop up.

Volunteer Rating System: Savvy volunteers devise an organizational rating system based on experiences with volunteer organizations. The star rating system awards stars for meaningful experience, timely placement, recognition and support. Organizations with the highest ratings use their star status in recruiting volunteers, applying for grants and attracting donors.

Volunteer Metrics: A central agency analyzes volunteer programs and experiments with algorithms to measure the impact of volunteering on societal challenges.

Volunteer Decentralization: Decentralized volunteers work in block chain technology. Instead of each organization owning their volunteers, the decentralized volunteers are free to move from one organization to another. Volunteers also post absences on a shared board, opening up the vacancy to other decentralized volunteers, thus removing the burden from a volunteer manager to find replacements.

Leaders of Volunteer Engagement and Impact Association: LoVEIA becomes the international agency lobbying for volunteer engagement professionals. It supports all other volunteer management associations and standardizes volunteer management through common terms, practices and the institution of a volunteer management support hotline.

MS Volunteer Management: A prestigious university offers a master's level degree in volunteer engagement. It begins as an offshoot of the Master's in Public Administration degree but is so popular due to the requirement that CEOs have volunteer management experience that a stand-alone degree is created.

Volunteer Robots: Companion robots become caregivers for people who are ill, infirmed and aging. Some volunteer managers move into programing the companion robots as companies look for ways to provide robots who mimic human caring with realistic volunteer phrases and skills.

Volunteer Biometrics: Volunteers sign into their activities via retinal scan. Based on DNA tests, volunteers are matched to experiences suited to their temperament.

Volunteer Credit Hours: Organizations offer credits for volunteering. Healthcare institutions give credits for hospital stays, educational entities offer credits for scholarships, etc. Companies looking to increase their corporate social responsibility jump on the bandwagon and offer points for volunteers to spend on products and services.

The Volunteer Club Trilogy: A series of books for young adults centers on a group of preteens who volunteer at a local volunteer organization. The club members solve mysteries while experiencing the angst of typical preteens. One of the central adult characters is the volunteer manager Hope, a crime show fan who helps the club members solve crimes. The success of the series spawns a whole new literary awareness of volunteers and main character volunteers appear in many genres.

Physician Prescribed Volunteering: The overwhelming evidence showing volunteerism is good for one's wellbeing spurs physicians into prescribing a volunteer activity. Leaders of volunteers report progress back to the physician through a clinical care plan. This movement expands into mental health entities, juvenile services and elder affairs.

Volunteer Influencers: High-profile volunteers become spokespersons for products, joining the ranks of famous athletes and media stars.

Volunteer Agency: Volunteer agencies, a hybrid of temporary employment agencies, run by leaders of volunteers pop up. Dedicated volunteer managers train and mentor volunteers and then place developed volunteers with organizations.

Grants from the private sector fund the agencies. As these agencies report on the increased wellbeing, readiness for employment and skill enhancement, funding pours in.

Volunteer Background Checks: After a retired U.S. senator attempts to volunteer at two places simultaneously and is forced to do two screenings on the same day, she lobbies to change laws allowing volunteer agencies to share background information subject to the consent of the volunteer. Screening becomes centralized and shared for seamless volunteer onboarding. Volunteers receive a card, much like a driver's license that confirms their background check has been completed.

Volunteer Marathon: Much like the telethon raising money over a weekend, the volunteer marathon uses social media to record hundreds of thousands of volunteering events and hours in real time over a weekend span.

Volunteering Hotlines: An executive in the communications industry institutes a hotline after he has trouble finding a volunteer activity for his team. His corporation funds the hotline, which is at first manned by employees and then, eventually volunteers.

Volunteer DNA: Popular DNA tracking companies add linking ancestry to famous past volunteers.

Interactive Volunteer Websites: Volunteering websites use chat bots that interact with prospective volunteers. Volunteers stand by to answer questions in real time.

Volunteer Data Systems: A software engineer, who had a life changing experience while volunteering, engineers a sophisticated data system that not only tracks prospective volunteers, volunteer hours, it also tracks fluid volunteer availability, volunteer skills and preferences, volunteer tasks offered and responses, training and future goals. (This frees up volunteer managers to rule the world!) Just kidding, but it does free up time to spend building innovative initiatives.

Augmented Reality: Prospective volunteers take an organizational tour and hear a thank you from a client or see volunteers at work through an augmented reality app. Recruitment skyrockets.

Volunteer Program Tag Lines: Volunteer programs are so popular, they stand apart from their host organizations with their own identity and taglines.

The first tagline comes from a leader of volunteers who works for a small disaster recovery organization. Her volunteer program's tagline is, "where passion meets results." Since the first tagline, thousands spring up, including "when you love it, it's not work," and "where actions impact everyone."

Career Development: Volunteer manager people skills catch the attention of an employment agency executive who hires several volunteer managers as consultants. A franchise, aptly named, "Coaching for Quality, the Volunteer Way" opens up in cities across the globe. Their most popular course, "Empathy, Energy and Employment," sells out in cities worldwide.

The Volunteerette television show: Modeled after popular dating shows, the volunteerette looks for a place to make a difference. Courted by organizations, the volunteerette tries each opportunity, sometimes with hilarious results and in the finale, she chooses the winning organization.

Volunteer memes: Volunteers in memes pop up. People use them to denounce mean people, slackers, arrogant people and the uninvolved. One popular meme is a picture of a volunteer drying the tears of a crying child. The words, "you wish you were this good," complete the meme.

●

While it's fun to fantasize, I hope you will take a moment and close your eyes. Envision what you imagine the future will hold. Be as creative and out of the box as possible. What if volunteerism was the most important component in a non-profit world? What if non-profit leaders first looked to the volunteer services department for solutions? What new ideas, no matter how "out there," might achieve this future?

These imaginative sparks hold the key. Inside each idea lies a blueprint for our journey forward. Think about what volunteering can look like if we work together to make it happen.

The future of volunteerism rests in the capable hands of each leader of volunteers. We are not alone. We are no longer isolated. We no longer have to feel as though we're the only ones who recognize the system is outdated. We all know how much volunteering matters to a civilized society. We know how much has been done, but we also know there is so much more we can accomplish if we are given the opportunity.

It won't be easy because we have work to do. We must disrupt the system so today's volunteers have the support they need to succeed. The knowledge and experience we possess is the key to demonstrating our immense potential.

It is up to us to take the steps necessary to enact change by first rethinking ourselves and changing our methods of showing volunteer value, then moving forward to create a new normal, one that organizations will be excited to embrace.

By becoming proactive in updating our volunteer engagement and impact programs, we will determine volunteerism's future. The work we do now to elevate our initiatives will pave the way for more meaningful volunteer roles and more respect and demand for volunteer contributions.

Linear thinking no longer attracts the modern volunteer. Meaningful engagement and showing value and impact is the future. Becoming leaders is the future. Sustaining volunteers is the future. Setting mission centric priorities is the future. .

It is a bright future. Volunteer managers are coming out of the non-profit shadows and claiming a rightful spot at the center of mission goals by engaging in mission centric volunteerism.

Let's lead this movement by reframing volunteer management into volunteer engagement and impact. Let's redefine volunteer managers as leaders of volunteers.

Let's reframe our priorities to meet the changing needs of our programs. Let's reshape non-profit culture to embrace our vision of volunteer engagement and impact. Let's cultivate volunteer sustainability. Let's take charge and believe in ourselves.

We can do this, step by step, so volunteer engagement is stronger for our determination to see it thrive and grow. We can move our programs forward if we band together.

Volunteer managers do not seek personal gain. Instead, we strive to share the gift of volunteer effectiveness with a world that sees possibilities in the ways we see it. We look to make a real difference.

We have a noble purpose and when we keep that purpose at the center of everything we say and do, we will succeed. Purpose gives us power, the power of a shared commitment to advance volunteerism and shape its direction.

I sincerely hope you have found ideas on these pages that will work for you. I hope in some way this book has inspired you to realize that you hold your future in your capable hands.

Thank you for all you do and thank you for reading my book.

-Meridian

Made in the USA
Monee, IL
16 January 2022